CARRILLO ADOBE BEFORE RESTORATION

*T*his mule-riding gaucho posed at the site of the Carrillo adobe located at ll East Carrillo Street in Santa Barbara while a part of the building still served as a dentist's office. It was built in the early Mexican period by Daniel Hill, a Massachusetts man who became an American citizen, marrying Rafaela Luisa Ortega y Olivera, daughter of Francisco Ortega, first commandante of the Santa Barbara Presidio.

When Seamaster John Wilson of Dundee, Scotland married Ramona Carrillo de Pacheco, widow of Captain Romualdo Pacheco, Wilson purchased this property. The year was 1836. By 1844, Wilson retired from the sea and the couple moved to their rancho, the Canada de los Osos, a few miles from the San Luis Obispo Mission settlement.

Ramona's sons by her former marriage, Romualdo and Mariano, were educated in a missionary school in the Sandwich Islands. Romualdo Pacheco became the twelth governor of California in the American period.

This property now belongs to the Santa Barbara Foundation. It is open to visitors on a daily basis.

Photo-Courtesy of the Santa Barbara Historical Society.

Loren Nicholson's
OLD PICTURE POSTCARDS
A Historic Journey Along California's Central Coast

This book commissioned by ARMAND ZOLEZZI

Graphics by TOMAS ZAZUETA

Cover by BERNICE NICHOLSON

COVER POSTCARDS: Mission Santa Barbara novitiate on portico and beach buggy at Pismo Beach with tent city in background.
BACK COVER: Along El Camino Real at Gaviota Pass.

Library of Congress Catalog Numbers: F 869-S35-N5-1989, F 869-S45-N5-1989, NC 1870-N5-1989
Published By CALIFORNIA HERITAGE PUBLISHING ASSOCIATES–San Jose, San Luis Obispo

No.1044 Santa Barbara, Cal.- S. P. Depot.   "Turrill & Miller Photo."

c. 1910— SOUTHERN PACIFIC DEPOT— A Special excursion train ran from San Luis Obispo and cities to the south for day visitors during this historic occasion.

SANTA BARBARA'S GREATEST CELEBRATION

"S anta Barbara's most glorious day has been recorded in the pages of history," the old Morning Press reported afterward. "Never (have) such throngs lined our boulevards and thoroughfares; never (have) such spectacles been witnessed by such enthusiastic crowds. The day has come and gone, but the story will last forever."

Actually, the "day" was more like three days. The newspaper referred to that breathless time beginning about 4:30 p.m. Sunday, April 26, 1908 when 16 ships of the Great White Fleet, the North Atlantic Division of the U.S. Navy, dropped anchor in the

THE GREAT WHITE FLEET— Two of the 16 U.S. Navy ships that anchored in the bay at Santa Barbara April 26, 1908.

Potter Hotel, front view, Santa Barbara, Cal.

POTTER HOTEL— Ground breaking for this luxurious hotel on the beach occurred January 19, 1902, Milo Potter's birthday. Potter celebrated his next birthday with the hotel's grand opening in 1903. He hung 10,000 lights on the exterior of the building as part of the festivities when the Great White Fleet came to Santa Barbara.

bay at Santa Barbara. The people of the Central Coast had been waiting months for this occasion. But no one worked harder or prepared more completely for these days than Milo Potter, owner of the Potter Hotel located at the beach.

The Panama Canal was not yet complete, so when the Atlantic fleet was ordered to join forces with the Pacific fleet, it made its way through the Antartica winds and bitter cold of the Strait of Magellan at the tip of South America to call at Pacific ports of South America, Mexico and the Pacific Coast of the United States. It would join forces with the Pacific fleet at San Francisco.

The Navy had accepted Santa Barbara's invitation to visit the city while en-route to San Francisco, and now, the people of the Central Coast enjoyed their days of glory and national attention, entertaining and being entertained.

There was only one disappointment. Rear Admiral Robley Evans became seriously ill even before the fleet reached San Diego. From this city, he was whisked by train to the El Paso de Robles Hot Springs Hotel, and his family joined him there. As daily reports about the Admiral's condition were made to the press, Paso Robles also found itself a center of national attention. During this time, the fleet came under command of Rear Admiral Charles Thomas.

The City of Santa Barbara had begun preparations for the navy's arrival at the beginning of April, so its citizens were ready. With throngs of people crowding the beach and every vantage point, Mayor Elmer Boeseke and members of the Civic Committee, including Milo Potter, rode out into the bay in a yacht to the Flagship Connecticut to welcome Rear Admiral Thomas and his staff to Santa Barbara's celebration.

But first, the people of Santa Barbara witnessed the light show of their lives. That evening, "Every vessel was outlined in fire," the Press reported. "Thousands of incandescent bulbs were strung along the deck lines, up the military masts, out the signal yard arms and up and down the funnels. Lights shone from bow to stern from all of the vessels in the bay."

The name of each ship was spelled in lighted letters six feet high across its forward bridge. But that was not spectacular enough

for the navy. For at least a half hour, they conducted a searchlight display, lights from individual ships crossing each other in a profusion of patterns.

Milo Potter made sure his hotel on the beach also had its show. Some 10,000 incandescent lights operated by the hotel's own power plant shone back at the ships in all their splendor while people crowded the gardens and took in the sights from lobby and room windows.

The Potter, the Arlington and all of the boarding houses were booked to capacity for this historic event. Special Southern Pacific trains operated to and from San Luis Obispo and Ventura Counties to bring day visitors, and the fleet opened several of its ships to public viewing, operating launches to and from shore.

Admiral Charles Thomas and the prin-

POTTER HOTEL— December 8, 1906— Swimmers at Santa Barbara with hotel in background.

cipal officers of the fleet enjoyed an experience unlike anything ever offered them on the East coast. When the time came for the parade, they were invited aboard the official carriage to ride to the viewing stand. It was a mountain coach covered with thousands of roses, carnations and cornflowers. The carriage was driven by the city's oldest Spanish family, the de la Guerras, all dressed in full costume of the Spanish-Mexican period in California.

Senorita Ynez de la Guerra Diblee was crowned queen of the festival by Admiral Thomas. She rode in a beautiful flower-decorated coach with other members of the Guerra family. Senorita Diblee had trained 40 dancers for the dance of the flowers planned the next day, and she, herself, would play a leading role on stage.

The parade included some sixty flower-decorated wagons and coaches, equestrian groups, marching bands from neighboring communities, and a marching navy contingent. American flags were everywhere, patriotic music swelled the air. People fairly shivered with pride for their country.

The officers' ball at the Potter Hotel hosted by Mrs. Milo Potter was "one of the most memorable ever known in the history of Santa Barbara," the newspaper reported. "It was a picture of such courtly brightness as is found in paintings of scenes in palaces of the old world."

When the fleet continued sailing up the coast, Admiral Thomas made a special effort to stay close enough to shore so that spectators who gathered on the beaches and bluffs at Pismo, Avila and Cambria could enjoy the sight of all 16 vessels plowing toward San Francisco. Some ships made stops at both Monterey and Santa Cruz. Eventually, the combined fleet of both oceans would show off at ports in Australia, New Zealand and other areas of the Pacific.

It was all part of President Theodore Roosevelt's foreign policy strategy. "Speak softly," he said, "and carry a big stick.

Castle Rock from Hotel Potter, Santa Barbara, Cal.

VERANDA of the Potter Hotel looking across lawns toward the bay. Note the many stout oak rockers.

ARLINGTON HOTEL— Established in downtown Santa Barbara in 1875 by a stock company headed by Col. William W. Hollister of Glen Annie Ranch. Its guest register was signed by famous people world-wide. It was destroyed by fire in 1809 and then rebuilt as an even larger finer hotel. It was finally destroyed in the 1925 earthquake as shown in another story in this book.

A VIEW OF SANTA BARBARA during the Mexican period as depicted by Alfred Robinson. Shows presidio with adobe casas around it. Mission visible on hill to left side.

RESTAURANTE EL PASEO, Santa Barbara— Featuring Mexican food and entertainment, the El Paseo was a favorite tourist attraction. These 1930's postcard photos by Karl Obert show a 1930's audience enjoying the ambiance as well as the entertainment. The restaurant was part of a much larger building with many shops located in back of Casa de la Guerra.

SUNDAY AT THE BEACH and Plaza del mar in Santa Barbara. People on the bluff in foreground enjoy the sun and a view of the long beach, the boulevard with its many palms and the expansive lawns of Hotel Potter .

EARLY BREAKWATER— When the tide was low, it made an enjoyable place to walk along the water in Santa Barbara.

The Sewing Room, Santa Barbara Mission, Cal.   *Copyright by G.P.Thresher, 1899.*

SEWING ROOM, MISSION SANTA BARBARA, 1899— Turn-of-the-century noviates posed for this photo depicting the early disciplined life of the priesthood. By this date, the Chumash Indian settlement, the tannery, the gristmill and the lavanderia, (the clothes washing area) had deteriorated. The mission now served as a parish church and college for young men training for the priesthood.

CALIFORNIA'S FIRST BISHOP SERVED IN SANTA BARBARA

*W*hen the scarred and gray Mexican sailing brig Guipuzcoana dropped anchor off the beach at Santa Barbara on January 11, 1841, every one in the pueblo who could walk or ride a horse gathered at the water's edge for the celebration.

Alfred Robinson, an American who held Mexican citizenship papers and lived in Santa Barbara, witnessed the whole event. "All was bustle," he wrote. "Men, women and children hastening to the beach, banners flying, drums beating and soldiers marching. The whole population of the place turned out to pay homage to this first bishop of California."

From the beach Santa Barbarans watched sailors aboard the brig drop a surfboat to the water and scramble down a rope ladder to assist their distinguished guest as he climbed over the side for the ride to shore.

As the surfboat neared shore, men rushed out into the water and pulled it through the wash of waves onto the beach. Then Bishop Francisco Garcia Diego y Moreno stepped ashore, and was "welcomed by a kneeling multitude," Robinson said. "All

5005. Mission Santa Barbara, California; founded in 1786.

MISSION SANTA BARBARA— Founded December 4, and dedicated December 16, 1786. The original mission was destroyed by an earthquake in 1812. The new mission was again damaged in the earthquake of 1826.

received his benediction; all kissed the pontifical ring."

A carriage waited, and soon took California's first bishop along the crooked trail that would one day be called State street. As he waved to those who waited along the trail and those who followed him, he undoubted saw the falling presidio that still housed a few soldiers and served as a symbolic defense against enemies. Past small whitewashed adobes, he was taken to the plaza and the large adobe-walled residence of Don Jose de la Guerra y Noriega.

Here, he lunched with the longstanding titular leader of the pueblo, Don Jose, served by Indian servants led by Antonia, his wife, and his several daughters. Meanwhile, people crowded around the gate waiting another opportunity to see this new man of God. It was a great moment. Of all the missions and pueblos in California, Bishop Garcia had chosen to make his headquarters in Santa Barbara.

When the Bishop reappeared in his carriage for the short trip to the mission, he wore colorful pontifical robes. Now, Robinson reported, heavy artillery in the presidio thundered its welcome. Men on horseback rode alongside his carriage playing guitars, violins and flutes. All of this attention must have been deeply satisfying to the Bishop.

This trip to California was not his first. In 1833, he had come as prefect in charge of a group of Zacatecan missionaries. He served at Mission Santa Clara for a year, then returned to Mexico seeking help for the California mission cause. During his short visit the first time, he witnessed the secularization of the northern California missions and probably realized the inevitable downfall of all of the others unless they were somehow rescued by Mexico. Today, he returned as the new leader of the catholic church in California. He had been promised control of California's share of the Pious Fund, as well as a large annual stipend for himself along with the right to seek tithing from California's catholics.

Garcia's biographers say that he visualized the development of many new missions and the construction of a beautiful cathedral at Santa Barbara, but he would soon learn, as the Fernandinos before him, that the government of Mexico gave little time or attention to their faraway California outposts. Nothing he tried during the next few years proved fruitful. Not even the congregation of his own church was generous in its tithing. Grievously disappointed, he died in April, 1846, only a few months before the American navy occupied Monterey and San Francisco.

Santa Barbara Mission Portico.

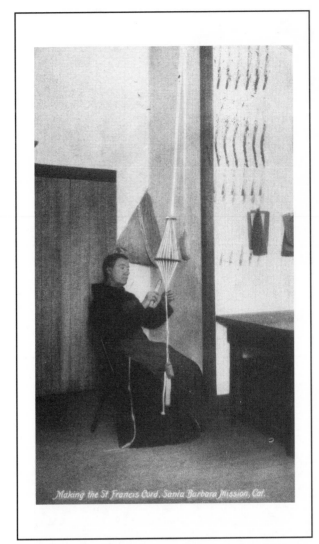

1910— A BROTHER of the novitiate exhibits skill as craftsman.

A REMINDER of Santa Barbara's annual Fiesta.

1910— Interior of Mission Santa Barbara.

Black-
smith
Shop,
Mission
Santa
Barbara,
Cal.

*1906— MISSION Santa Barbara black-
smith shop. A brother of the novitiate poses
with hammer over anvil for this postcard.*

Datura Tree, or Angels Trumpet
— In the Gardens of Santa
Barbara Mission, California.

*1910— PRIEST MEDITATES under an
Angels Trumpet tree in the Santa Barbara
Mission Garden.*

FAMOUS HOME OF CAPTAIN JOSE de la Guerra y Noriega and his wife Antonio, daughter of Raimundo Carrillo. Guerra was commandante of the Santa Barbara presidio and acted on behalf of Central Coast missions in business affairs. He retired from the military in 1842, but was viewed as Santa Barabara's patriarch until he died in 1858. His four daughters all married Americans.

THIS OLD STONE high school building served many generations in Santa Barbara before it was replaced. Streets had not yet been paved when this postcard was made.

HIGHLIGHTS IN THE HISTORY OF
MISSION SANTA BARBARA

SEPTEMBER 6, 1772- Padre Junipero Serra, traveling with Commandante Pedro Fages, arrives at site of present City of Santa Barbara.

APRIL 2, 1782- Santa Barbara Presidio founded by Governor Felipe de Neve, Padre Junipero Serra and Captain Jose Francisco de Ortega, first commandante of the presidio.

DECEMBER 4, 1786- Mission Santa Barbara founded. Padre Fermin Francisco Lasuen, third presidente of the growing California chain of missions, presides over the dedication ceremonies.

1788- As Indian converts increase in number, the original chapel is enlarged.

1789- Construction of a second church begins.

1797- A third mission church of adobe construction was started.

1797- The chapel at the presidio is completed and consecrated.

1802- Five large tanning vats and thirty-five new adobe houses built.

1806- Padre Ripoll overseas construction of first reservoir for the Santa Barbara settlement.

1807- Indians build a dam for the mission under direction of the Franciscan fathers.

December 21. 1812- Earthquake destroys Mission Santa Barbara.

September 10, 1820- A new mission church is completed and dedicated at ceremonies with Goveror Pablo Vicente de Sola, Santa Barbara Presidio Commandante Jose de la Guerra and troops of the presidio taking part.

April, 1822- Santa Barbara takes oath of alligiance to the new Republic of Mexico and lowers the flag of Spain.

February 22, 1824- Santa Barbara Indians revolt against soldiers. Several lives are lost.

August 17, 1833- The Congress of Mexico decrees secularization of California Missions, freeing mission rancho lands and Indian neophytes from church jurisdiction.

April 27, 1840- Padre Francisco Garcia Diego y Moreno appointed California's first bishop.

January 11, 1842- The Bishop establishes his residence at Santa Barbara Mission.

April, 1846- Bishop Garcia Diego y Moreno dies and is buried at Mission Santa Barbara, just a few months before the American take over of California.

August 4-5, 1846- American forces anchor at Santa Barbara and take city, leaving a small garrison in charge. The American flag raised in the pueblo.

December 27, 1846- John C. Fremont and his volunteers arrive in Santa Barbara enroute to Los Angeles.

May 31, 1872- Four leagues of pueblo land conferred to the City of Santa Barbara by President Ulysses S. Grant.

1901- Santa Barbara Mission dedicates St. Anthony's College to prepare young men for the priesthood.

1925- The mission is severely damaged by the earthquake. Restoration undertaken the next year.

TURN-OF-CENTURY MAY DAY CELEBRANTS

So many traditional holidays of earlier years have been tempered in our day. May Day is one of these events. While it continues as an important holiday in some countries, it does not receive nearly as much attention on the Central Coast of California as it did in the early part of the century.

These San Luis Obispo ladies pose for a group portrait on the lawn of the Robert E. Jack and Gertrude Hollister Jack residence on Marsh Street following a parade and their "dance of the flowers." In Santa Barbara, a similar group led by Senorita Ynez de la Guerra Diblee had entertained while the Great White Fleet was in port in 1908.

May Day was so important that girls thought about it and worked on their dresses for weeks ahead. They also attended several dance rehearsals. The floral garlands that framed their heads borrow from medieval Europe when the carrying in procession of trees, green branches and garlands was part of celebrating spring. The day traditionally included a May king and queen and the set-ting up of a May tree or Maypole. In pre-Christian times, these rites were intended to insure fertility of crops as well as cattle and human beings.

The Jack residence where the girls celebrated was constructed in the 1880's while Jack was active in banking, land develop-ment and local politics. He served as mayor of San Luis Obispo, officer and board mem-ber of the West Coast Land Company and board member or officer of several county banks. Jack's largest personal land holding was the 27,000-acre Cholame Rancho in the Northeastern part of San Luis Obispo County. This property was originally granted to Mauricio Gonzales by Mexican governor Manuel Micheltorena in 1844.

The Jack residence was given to the City of San Luis Obispo in recent times. Much of the house is furnished with late nineteenth century victorian furniture. Tours are regularly conducted by the Jack House docents, and the gardens are available for rent by groups.

Loren Nicholson's

OLD PICTURE POSTCARDS

A Historic Journey Along California's Central Coast

This book commissioned by
ARMAND ZOLEZZI

Graphics by
TOMAS ZAZUETA

Cover by
BERNICE NICHOLSON

COVER POSTCARDS: Mission Santa Barbara novitiate on portico and beach buggy at Pismo Beach with tent city in background.

BACK COVER: Along El Camino Real at Gaviota Pass.

SAN LUIS OBISPO COUNTY

SANTA BARBARA COUNTY

Library of Congress Catalog Numbers: F 869-S35-N5-1989, F 869-S45-N5-1989, NC 1870-N5-1989
Published By CALIFORNIA HERITAGE PUBLISHING ASSOCIATES–San Jose, San Luis Obispo

HOTEL RAMONA— Opened October 3, 1888. Both this hotel and the new El Paso de Robles Hotel which opened October 12, 1891 were constructed in anticipation of new business with the arrival of the Southern Pacific Railroad.

PRESIDENT WILLIAM McKINLEY SPEAKS ON CENTRAL COAST

*I*n our yesteryears, the Central Coast rated visits by several presidents of the United States, and they received the grandest possible treatment. Take, for example, President William McKinley's orations from the verandas of the Arlington Hotel in Santa Barbara and the Ramona Hotel in San Luis Obispo in May, 1901. He was the first president to visit either city.

In Santa Barbara, President McKinley spoke under draped flags from the steps of the Arlington on State Street. After his presentation to a cheering happy audience, he continued to San Luis Obispo. The Southern Pacific Railroad had completed track between Surf and Ellwood near Santa Barbara only 10 days earlier, making this trip by train possible.

At 7 o'clock that evening the San Luis Obispo reception committee greeted the president at the station and escorted him to a floral-decorated carriage prepared by the newly organized women's group called the Twentieth Century Club.

People owning the classiest carriages in town joined the President and his men in an entourage along Santa Rosa Street, then East along Higuera Street to the Ramona Hotel.

At the entrance to the hotel grounds the veterans of the Civil War, members of the Fred Steele Post and the Colonel Harper Post of the Grand Army of the Republic "were drawn up" to salute their commander-in-chief as he passed.

"Midst deafening cheers," the San Luis Obispo Tribune said, the President took his place on the hotel veranda, and Mayor Shipsey introduced him.

President McKinley had been elected to his second term in 1900. He was viewed as a tough-minded man, and there were many issues about which he could have talked. While a Congressman from Ohio, he sponsored the highly protective McKinley Tariff Act to stop importation of foreign goods. He first ran for president on the issue of maintaining a strict gold standard currency. In 1898, he urged the favorable vote of the legislature in declaring war upon Spain, and in the peace settlement, he took Cuba, Puerto Rico and the Phillippines for this country. He also signed the bill that annexed Hawaii to the United States and supported an open door policy with China.

But he did not speak about any of these issues during his visit in Santa Barbara or San Luis Obispo. He talked about the warm welcome given him, and he acknowledged the men of the G.A.R. He talked of the gallantry and courage of fighting men in the Civil War and the Spanish-American War. His audiences in both communities beamed with patriotism, cheering him to even greater oration.

When he finished speaking in San Luis Obispo, Miss Mary Hollister, the daughter of John H. Hollister, came to his side with a large basket of flowers and gifts. Among other things, the basket included an album of photos of the area, a painting of Mission San Luis Obispo on celluloid, some locally written poems and a "macate" made from six shades of human hair. It was a memorable moment for Mary, and the President seemed genuinely touched.

His train had now moved into position in back of the hotel. From the rear platform of his parlor car, he continued shaking hands with all comers until the train slowly pulled away for San Francisco.

Five months later, President McKinley was shot dead in Buffalo, New York by Leon Czolgosz. He died in the hospital from his wounds on September 14, 1901, and Vice President Theodore Roosevelt became the country's next president. Two years later, President Roosevelt came to California, visiting and speaking in Santa Barbara and San Luis Obispo.

PRESIDENT WILLIAM McKINLEY, under hanging flag, speaks to Santa Barbara audience from veranda of New Arlington Hotel.

St. Siena in San Luis Obispo, Cal.

MONTEREY STREET at the turn of the century. Horses, buggies prevailed. Streets were dusty in summer and muddy in winter. Sinsheimer's metal-fronted building on the right.

STREETS, LANES, AND ALLEYS IN OLD SAN LUIS OBISPO

Come tour a few of the early lanes and alleys of the old San Luis Obispo settlement in the 1870's and later. There were no postcards during those years except the ones we can conger up in our imaginations.

For example, it would be such a pleasure to see a picture postcard of the old Priests' Lane shown on the old 1870 map. This lane was almost a streetwide swatch of land starting in front of the mission, running down and up the slopes of the creek and then, continuing through what would probably be the present-day Network building to reach Higuera street. The lane led to the mission vineyards which also showed on the old city map. What photo buff wouldn't like a picture of one of the early priests strolling or riding a mule from the mission to the vineyard.

Of course, it would be equally exciting to have an early picture postcard of some of the activity in the vineyard. Say, a group of Chumash Indian boys and girls picking grapes. Our map identifies the greater part of the city limits south of Higuera street as "Mission Vineyard." When this land was finally subdivided in 1874 and legally transferred by the church in April, 1875, to individual owners, the street in the vineyard almost opposite Priests' Lane was named Garden Street. This street, then only a trail, provided entrance into the vineyards. What a nice heritage for a city street.

During the early years of shaping this settlement into a town and finally a city there was no Chorro street running between Monterey and Higuera, but there was a trail which was called Spring Lane that led from either direction so that wagons could ford Arroyo de San Luis Obispo, the city's creek. In 1874, the city trustees contracted to level a street through that block and build a bridge that cost $1,323. They built another bridge across Chorro Street farther north where Stenner Creek crossed. This opened the Chorro trail, the "road from San Luis Obispo to Cambria," according to the contract. I wish I had a picture of drovers running cattle across those bridges and out the Chorro trail, even though local people complained about this happening in town at some seasons of the year.

Lovers of local history might also enjoy an old picture postcard showing farmers watering their horses in San Luis Obispo creek at the end of Rose Alley. This wayward lane still runs alongside the Sinsheimer Store off Monterey Street. The late Elliot Curry, a Tribune reporter and much-loved writer of local history once described a trial that occurred in 1907 concerning the legal ownership of the alley. The case was appealed all of the way to the state supreme court to establish the city's ownership. The decision in favor of the city still stands.

As long as I'm wishing, I wish we had a postcard of San Luis Obispo's first courthouse, a two-story adobe house constructed by William Goodwin Dana on the south side

MONTEREY STREET LOOKING NORTH, SAN LUIS OBISPO, CALIFORNIA   704

© STANLEY A. PILTZ   9A-H2635

MONTEREY STREET, early forties. Sinsheimers on right. Anderson Hotel in the distance.

HIGUERA AND CHORRO STREETS, 1918— "Dear sister, Tim and I were married this afternoon."

HIGUERA STREET, 1930's— On right, Security First National Bank, Wineman Hotel.

Street Scene in San Luis Obispo, Mission in the Distance

MONTEREY STREET, West of Mission— Card reads: "This is the street where we lived when Ella was born. I have made an 'x' where the same old house stands. The number '2' is the old mission, and '3' is old Dr. Hayes home, '4' is where uncle Frank lives. I think your Mama will know the Pepper Trees. I will send more cards of San Luis Obispo, (signed) Aunt R."

of Monterey street between Morro and Osos street along that part of the present-day parking lot once known as Court street. The 1870 map identifies this land as The Plaza. Once in 1867 while District Judge Pablo de la Guerra worked in La Casa Grande, the name given this courthouse, he wrote a letter to his wife in Santa Barbara describing what he saw and heard on The Plaza opposite the courthouse.

"This is written," he said, "in the midst of the noise and uproar of the children, men, oldsters and ladies watching the bullfight. With each turn or gore of the bull, there is a universal shout, and unfortunately, the house in which I write is in the very plaza where the celebration is occurring."

It was fiesta time in San Luis Obispo. Six priests participated in the mass that day, and there were two dances in the evening. Yes, I wish I had some picture postcards of the fiesta that took place that August 19, 1867, but no such cards exist. The cards described herein are but pictures in my head, although the places and events were real.

Court House, San Luis Obispo, Cal.

SAN LUIS OBISPO'S THIRD COURTHOUSE— When the County was established in 1850, the new government rented rooms in the mission for a records office, courtroom and jail. Within a few years, the court and records were moved to La Casa Grande, a two-story adobe structure owned by William Goodwin Dana at the corner of the early "Court" street on Monterey. During 1875, J.W. Andrews contributed land for construction of the above building. In 1940, it was replaced by today's much enlarged facility. The building in back became the records office.

SAN LUIS OBISPO'S second permanent library. The first library was established in rooms above the J.P. Andrews Bank at Monterey and Los Osos, on June 15, 1894. A grant from Andrew Carnegie in 1902 made the structure shown here possible . It became the San Luis Obispo County Historical Museum in February, 1956.

SOUTHERN PACIFIC ROUNDHOUSE in San Luis Obispo— The line reached the city on May 5, 1894. The brick roundhouse, the station and freight office were built during the months following.

THE CITY OF SAN LUIS OBISPO from Islay Hill. Immediately behind houses in foreground, the railroad depot and some boxcars are visible. The three-story red brick building is the Palm Hotel. Note the sparcity of houses. There were no houses on San Luis Mountain.

PICTURESQUE COSTUMES, CHINATOWN

SAN FRANCISCO'S CHINATOWN with children wearing oriental costumes.

EARLY CHINESE ALONG THE CENTRAL COAST

Next time you're nearby, take another look at that historic little brick building at the corner of Palm and Chorro Streets in San Luis Obispo called the Ah Louis Store.

Its modest 19th century stance, singularly isolated against the sky in the midst of the city, symbolizes the patient rise of not just a family but the whole population of Chinese in California.

San Francisco was the principal port of their arrival. They came to this city of promise at the same time and for the same reasons that Americans, Mexicans, Chileans, Peruvians, British, French, Germans and even Kanakans from the Sandwich Islands came. They came looking for gold.

However, they were not at all familiar to the others. They wore loose, wide-sleeved blouses and banded skull caps. Their dark hair hung in long queues. They didn't speak English, and their silence made them appear mysterious and aloof.

The rough-and-tumble and unenlightened men who made up the new California territory both feared and made fun of these differences, using the Chinese as scapegoats for their almost predatory intolerance.

"Of different language, blood, religion and character," Soule wrote in the Annals of San Francisco in 1854, "the Chinaman is looked upon by some as only a little superior to the negro, and by others as somewhat inferior."

The Chinese began to arrive in small numbers after the worldwide reports of the California gold strike in 1848. Then, in 1851 and 1852, so many came into San Francisco that they were conspicuous by their numbers. By 1854, there were some 10,000 Chinese in and around San Francisco. They were driven in and out of the mining regions. California Governor John Bigler added to the intolerance by trying to persuade the state legislature to pass a law forbidding further Chinese immigration. Soule reports that Governor Bigler's remarks were considered "offensive and uncalled for" by most intelligent Americans.

Many Chinese hired out in labor gangs for work in the gold mines. Both Chinese and Americans acted as labor bosses. These workers were treated like slaves, receiving subsistence and about $5 a month.

In San Francisco, they huddled together along the upper part of Sacramento Street and the length of Dupont to form the first Chinatown in the United States. Some of them became merchants, bringing in products from Canton. Many handwashed clothes for the white San Franciscans using various lagoons and wells in the developing city. They ironed clothes with a smooth-bottomed chafing dish filled with hot coals, and performed backbreaking jobs of any kind wherever they could be hired.

It was another decade before construction of the continental railroad provided jobs for all who were available and for many more still arriving.

Then, in the early 1870's, some of them began migrating to small towns in California, including San Luis Obispo, Santa Barbara and the other communities of the Central Coast. The 1870 census tells us that 59 Chinese had found their way into San Luis Obispo County. Ah Louis was one of them.

ESTABLISHED IN 1874 by Ah Louis, merchant and Chinese labor boss.

He built his two-story brick building on Palm Street in San Luis Obispo in 1874. Unpainted wooden buildings along that block served as housing and business locations for many of the others, establishing a Chinatown.

The old picture postcard showing the Ah Louis Store was given us by the late Young Louis, number one son of Ah Louis. It was published as part of the celebration of the store's centennial year in 1974.

In addition to selling merchandise during those first years, Ah Louis conducted a Chinese labor office. The Pacific Coast

Railway Company, the narrow gauge line running from Avila to San Luis Obispo and then to Arroyo Grande, Nipomo, Santa Maria, Los Alamos and Los Olivos, employed Chinese labor gangs during its years of constructing rail lines through northern Santa Barbara County. Ah Louis and his offspring became leaders and key citizens, contributing importantly to the city's development.

In their migration South, some Chinese settled in Santa Barbara. They were readily hired as household servants on the ranches and growing estates of the area. The going wage for their services at the end of the last century was $25 a month. Between 1870 and 1890, about 10% of Santa Barbara's population was Chinese. According to Thomas Storke in his book California Editor, the Chinese did most of the laundry in Santa Barbara.

Chinatown in Santa Barbara grew up in the general vicinity of the old presidio ruins. The hub of the district was where Canon Perdido intersects with Anacapa Street.

About 300 Chinese occupied the many adobe houses built during the Mexican period.

Both Santa Barbara and San Luis Obispo newspapers tell stories of the jubilant Chinese New Year celebrations. "My ears ring yet from the boom of giant firecrackers, the clash of gongs and cymbals and the thunder of skyrockets," Storke wrote. "How the Chinese quarter escaped wholesale conflagration, I do not know."

In February, 1883 the San Luis Obispo Tribune reported the same event in town. "Commencing at 3 p.m. our celestial friends kept up a deafening roar by letting off huge strings of firecrackers."

Townspeople came to Palm Street to enjoy the fun. "The devils were scared off," the Tribune reported, "and John (the name used to refer to the Chinese) will, for another year, pursue the even tenor of his way."

The Ah Louis Store, representing so much in our California heritage, enjoys the status of California Registered Historical Landmark No. 802.

1907— CHINESE children one year after San Francisco earthquake.

A STREET in San Francisco with Chinese fortune teller.

CHILDREN of Chinatown in San Francisco.

694 – CALIFORNIA POLYTECHNIC SCHOOL, NEAR SAN LUIS OBISPO, CALIFORNIA.

CALIFORNIA POLYTECHNIC STATE UNIVERSITY, c1913-From the beginning, Cal Poly was designated as a school to provide both "mental and manual training in the arts and sciences including agriculture, mechanics, engineering business methods, domestic economy" and other nonprofessional walks of life.

FOUNDING A UNIVERSITY

*I*n 1893, Cal Poly existed only as an idea in the mind of Myron Angel, an unusually public-spirited San Luis Obispo man.

The next year Angel wrote the district's new state senator, S.C. Smith, urging him to propose a normal school in the San Luis Obispo area to the state legislature. It was too late in the legislative sessions to take any action that year, but Angel had successfully planted his idea with Senator Smith.

Two years later Angel wrote a letter published in the San Luis Obispo Breeze hoping to enthuse the community, saying, "A normal school..can (add) to our fame and prosperity..the elegant buildings will be an ornament to the city. (The school can bring) professors and families of rank and education with hundreds of pupils of worthy ambition and refinement to our city..."

Several local men suggested that Angel call a public meeting. About twenty people attended. They elected Judge W.L. Beebee as chairman and County Clerk Whicher as secretary of a citizen's committee. Myron Angel, Mayor W.A. Henderson and T.K. Tuley agreed to prepare a petition for voter's signatures. From simply an idea, the future Cal Poly became a community project.

In 1897 Senator Smith took up the challenge, introducing a bill for a normal school at San Luis Obispo. But soon, a serious problem surfaced. San Diego had also petitioned for a normal school. Standing up to such competition seemed impossible.

A legislative delegation came to San Luis Obispo to evaluate the community's possibilities. Meantime, Senator Smith suggested that San Luis Obispo's leaders alter their request by asking for a state polytechnic school. This new objective would take them out of competition with larger cities. So, the local committee adjusted its aims and prepared to wine and dine the state committee.

The legislators arrived in town February 20, 1897. The city council voted $100 to host them.

"I have planned a school here that will teach the hand as well as the head," Angel told the group during a luncheon at the Ramona Hotel. The new polytechnic theme was underway. Other speakers that day included Judge E. P. Unangst, R. E. Jack, and School Superintendent N. Messer.

It was a truly impressive meeting. Back in Sacramento, both houses of the legislature voted in favor of developing a polytechnic school in San Luis Obispo. However, Governor Budd was concerned about budget. He vetoed the bill.

For a time, some people gave up hope, but Senator Smith presented his bill again in 1899. The Senate approved, but this time, the Assembly voted it down.

In 1901, Senator Smith tried again. By now, he had gained a great deal of experience in dealing with legislative matters. He succeeded in getting his bill on the floor early in both houses of the legislature, and San Luis Obispo sent a healthy delegation of leading citizens to Sacramento to talk to legislators. This time both houses and the governor approved the bill. At last, a polytechnic school would be built in San Luis Obispo.

Of course, most local people assumed the governor would appoint Myron Angel to the school's first board of trustees, but Angel belonged to the wrong political party.

In reporting the bill's passage, the San Luis Obispo Tribune said, "We must prepare and look forward to the day when the California Polytechnic School will become one of the great institutions of the State and the Pacific Coast."

Cal Poly opened its doors to its new student body of fifteen students on October 1, 1903. Today, nearly 16,000 young people attend the University.

CALIFORNIA POLYTECHNIC SCHOOL. SAN LUIS OBISPO. CALIFORNIA.
Science Building.

One of three buildings on the first campus, its uses changed many times. It was removed in recent years to make room for a new architecture building.

SAN MARCOS BUILDING— Three people were killed in the wreckage.

EARTHQUAKE IN SANTA BARBARA!

*P*eople all over town later reported that their animals began acting strangely. Cows and horses suddenly kicked and pranced, dogs began howling, chickens joined in a barnyard chorus and cats crouched in corners. The animals seemed to sense the impending danger.

Then the quake struck. The earth shifted in dizzying jerks, and people already beginning the day's business clung to whatever was nearest to keep their footing.

A 60,000 gallon water tank located in one of the towers of the New Arlington Hotel crashed through the building to ground level, crushing and killing Mrs. Charles Perkins, widow of the former president of the Chicago, Burlington and Quincy Railroad and

24-year-old Burton Hancock, both guests at the hotel. The entire frame of the San Marcos building collapsed, burying and killing building engineer S. Mostiero, orthodontist Dr. James Angio and an unknown woman. During the next several days, a dozen bodies would be found in the ruins.

Our photos come from a small souvenir-type booklet, each photo suitable for use as a postcard. Don Strassburg, a former resident of Santa Barbara, found them among family memoirs and shared them.

Thomas Storke, early publisher and editor of the Santa Barbara Press, called that fateful day of June 29, 1925 "Black Monday." The first tremor struck at 6:45 in the morning. It destroyed the old courthouse and county jail, the public library, the one-week-old Californian Hotel along with other downtown business buildings and residences. One of the towers of Mission Santa Barbara toppled and the other was badly cracked.

There was no power to operate the linotype machines nor the rotary press at the newspaper office, but Publisher Storke knew he must somehow publish an issue reporting this event. He and the mechanical superintendent entered the building that same morning and began handsetting type and arranging it in a page font. Even while people scurried about the city's ruins searching for injured, Storke searched the typecase for words of hope. "We..."are meeting the burdens of this calamity," he said, placing each metal letter one after the other into his composition stick. "The hand of the builder will soon begin the task of rebuilding." Using a hand-operated job shop press, Storke published a single page newspaper that day.

He ended his editorial with some very prophetic words: "..in the end," he told his readers, "Santa Barbara will come back bigger and stronger.." because "the men who built" the city "are still here."

It took the telephone company about 30 hours to restore local services, but much longer to bring back normal long distance calling. Anyone needing to make a long distance call could do so by using temporary phones set up in a shed in back of the telephone company building. A detail of about 150 boys delivered messages around town as calls came into the shed from worried relatives living elsewhere.

The city's spirited building trade council quickly adopted a resolution to cooperate in every possible way during the reconstruction of the city.

The front walls of the power plant of

POWER HOUSE of the Edison Company.

the street car company had fallen and buried the central generator that powered the street-cars, but the company rather quickly restored transportation by bringing in buses, a very modern idea. The courthouse had to be evacuated, and the Superior Court was moved into the nearby Farm Bureau building.

People welcomed the arrival of U.S. Navy ships in the bay. Crew members of the Battleship Arkansas, the coast guard cutter Tamaroa, the Destroyer McCauley and the Tug Koka came ashore to help patrol and contribute to relief work. The Salvation Army and the City Fire Department both set up food service centers, and the Red Cross took care of the homeless and needy. Police and firemen from Los Angeles arrived in town to serve as volunteer guards of the

AMERICAN LEGION HALL— Local military guard on duty. Building was a total loss.

*AUTOMOBILE
ROW RUINS*

open ruins.

Since so much damage had been done to the churches, a community service was held in Alameda Park that first Sunday morning after the earthquake.

When the dead had been properly mourned, the injured cared for, and the ruins of old Santa Barbara cleared, a few leaders in the city began expressing a special optimism. For some years, people who loved the city had felt that its architecture and construction had gone awry. It was losing its special Spanish-Meditteranean roots. Out of the chaos, a citizen's group formed to considered the future.

The Santa Barbara Press quoted enthusiastic citizens who spoke at one of the meetings. "Here is Santa Barbara's golden opportunity to carry out plans for city improvement..(using)..the beautiful Spanish style architecture represented about the plaza and on State and Carrillo Streets," one said.

"Let us here and now take our opportunity to make Santa Barbara the most beautiful individualized city in America," someone else said.

"Let us..adopt a definite architectural treatment in the reconstruction of the business (buildings)..the Spanish and Meditteranean type of design."

It was the beginning of something wonderful. By 1929, the new courthouse was completed. Its massive Spanish-Moorish architecture became an inspiration in designing a building code for the whole city. Its interior murals and Tunisian tile attracted so many tourists that organized tours of the building are still conducted several days a week.

Out of that disastrous earthquake of 1925, came the codes for a uniform architectural style that guides the city today. Most visitors agree that the inspiration of Santa Barbara's citizens committees of those years established the ground work for making their city one of the most beautiful in the world.

RUINS OF the County Jail.

NEW ARLINGTON AFTER earthquake— One tower held a 60,000 gallon water tank which crashed through the ground floor killing two guests while they slept.

ABOVE: ESTADO at De la Guerra Street.   BELOW: VAN NESS Hotel on Ortega Street.

ABOVE: FIRST National Bank   *BELOW: SANTA BARBARA public library*

1000 – HALL OF RECORDS AND COURT HOUSE, SANTA BARBARA, CALIFORNIA.

UNTIL SANTA BARBARA'S EARTHQUAKE in June, 1925, these buildings served as the Hall of Records and the Court House. Their destruction led to inspired new building codes and the Spanish-Mediterranean architecture so prominent in the city now.

COMPLETION OF track from Saugus into Santa Barbara occurred in the summer of 1887, and the first train arrived August 19. It ran through Fillmore, Santa Paula and Ventura, actually tying to the Valley line operating between Los Angeles and San Francisco.

No. 1044 Santa Barbara, Cal.- S. P. Depot.   "Terrill & Miller Photo."

LOS BANOS del MAR (the baths by the sea), one of the finest salt water natatoriums in the country facing a beautiful little plaza adjourning the beach. Here a crowd gathers to enjoy an afternoon concert.

On the Beach, Pacific Coast.
2nd Point, Santa Barbara, Cal.

1908— AROUND THE POINT at the beach in Santa Barbara.

1911-CABRILLO STREET at the beach— Potter Hotel in left background. The palm trees were small at the time. Here, horsedrawn carriages follow the boulevard while walkers stroll along the breakwater.

ON THE BEACH IN SANTA BARBARA— Note Stearn's Wharf in the distance. Bathhouse on far left with Potter Hotel in distance. Large numbers of people remained fully garbed during beach visits.

FIRST SIDEWALK in San Luis Obispo was asphalt laid in front of mission.

BISHOP MADE FIRST SIDEWALK IN SAN LUIS OBISPO POSSIBLE

*B*ishop Thaddeus Amat, in charge of the California diocese of the Catholic Church, introduced an exciting innovation in the care and maintenance of town walkways in San Luis Obispo during 1874.

He made $1600 available to the San Luis Obispo Mission Church for the express purpose of grading, excavating, curbing and paving a sidewalk between Chorro and Broad in front of the church. This sidewalk-wide stretch of asphalt paving was the first in San Luis Obispo.

What made this event especially meaningful to the townspeople was the knowledge that the "asphaltum" paving actually came from rock quarried in the vicinity of Edna Valley. Some years later, quarrying this rock became quite an industry in the area.

After the Pacific Coast Railway began

running through the valley, rock could be loaded and freighted to Harford's Wharf at Avila, where it was shipped on steam freighters to large cities for use in paving streets and sidewalks.

Tribune Editor R. S. Rembaugh noted that the sidewalk contractor, a Mr. Nuevall, had introduced "an entirely new feature into our town which promises to revolutionize the appearance of streets."

"It is really a treat to take a stroll now to the west end of town and to think that the mud and dust which used to characterize it are now laid to rest..." he wrote.

Residents and visitors alike walked the new walkway and marveled at its smoothness and levelness. Some people were seeing asphalt for the first time in their lives.

For sometime, editor Rembaugh had

complained about the twists, dips, falls and ruts in the streets of San Luis Obispo, but no one saw any immediate way to overcome the problem. As he said, "Unfortunately, the town was begun wrong. She needs..to be born again."

He was referring to the willy-nilly construction of earlier years before the town was laid out. The site had served well as a mission compound, but now residents hoped to develop a modern town with straight, wide streets and well-constructed bridges across the creek to accommodate buggy and wagon traffic.

"Above all things, let something like uniform sidewalks be at once laid down Monterey Street," Rembaugh urged. "At present, in the winter time, foot passage is not only uncomfortable but almost dangerous.

After dark, the only safe route for transit is the middle of the street."

For years, the creek without bridges hindered development and until 1870, the mission gardens consumed much of the land south of Higuera Street. After that date, the mission sold dozens of lots along and between the present-day Garden and Morro streets.

There are many pages of land transfers in the old books of the county recorders office during the 1870's showing sales by Bishop Amat, acting on behalf of the church.

The town trustees didn't take the idea of paved streets seriously until the new century and the automobile age, but they did lay "asphaltum" sidewalks on business streets during the next few years.

CONVENT—This building first served as a catholic boarding school for girls. Later, it was the residence for nuns of the church. It was destroyed by fire in 1930.

MISSION SAN LUIS OBISPO dated December 27, 1850— Depicts life in settlement the year California became a state.

LIFE IN A CALIFORNIA SETTLEMENT DURING THE 1850's

In 1887, Samuel A. Pollard, a long-time resident of San Luis Obispo County, wrote an article for the local Tribune about life as he lived it in the 1850's. It is a fascinating first-hand report of conditions as he remembered them.

*T*he good old days of the 50's now seem like a delightful dream to those who were then in California. Two of us came here (San Luis Obispo) to open a store.

Everyone had plenty of money even to the Indian vaquero, as the country was full of cattle, sheep and horses, and the miners in the north (the gold country) depended upon this part of California for their meat. So, we thought this a good place for a store and ours was the first opened.

Calico costing 12-1/2 cents per yard in San Francisco sold for cash at 50 cents here; sheeting was the same; all merchandise brought a good price.

Our goods were landed in surf boats. It was very dangerous and many lost their

1856— HENRY MILLER traveled through San Luis Obispo and left this interpretation of Mission San Luis Obispo architecture in his portfolio of sketches.

lives at this landing (Avila). Sometimes, a boat would be struck by a roller (wave) and lifted straight up, standing in the air on its bow, throwing it completely over and falling on some of the sailors.

Then if any of the crew got nervous and did not keep up his steady stroke, the boat would veer, get broadside with the roller and go over, burying them all under it.

Goods were frequently stolen as they reached the beach. Barrels of whiskey and bags of rice and sugar would be tumbled into a hole dug in the sand and hidden from sight.

Soon after our arrival in San Luis Obispo, we began building that now dirty looking old adobe relic at the corner of Monterey and Chorro Streets. Though now it looks shabby and forlorn and stands back from view as if ashamed of being found amid such handsome company, there was a day when the old pioneer surpassed anything in the county.

After we finished building the adobe, it was opened with a grand ball, the like of

1856— FROM A RISE, Henry Miller sketched Mission San Luis Obispo and the gardens. This garden area would become the business district of the city. The rock wall in foreground was included in early city maps.

1864—Edward Vischer prepared several sketches showing life in the Mission San Luis Obispo settlement. Here, he depicts a bullfighting contest. While one group fights the bull, another waits for a turn.

which had never before been seen in the county, and for years after, was spoken of by the Californians with pride as 'el baile grande de San Luis Obispo'.

All of the patriarchs of the county were there. They were the former owners of those immense estates which have nearly all left the hands of their descendants and are now furnishing so many happy homes to the newcomers.

There was old Captain John Wilson from England (actually Dundee, Scotland), a sea captain, then the owner of the Ranchos Osos and Laguna and Suey and Piedra Blanca; Captain Dana, the owner of the Nipomo Rancho; Mr. Branch, an old mountaineer, who after retiring from trapping and hunting through the Rocky Mountains, found his home in lovely California and was the owner of the Santa Manuela and Bolsa de Chamisal Ran-

chos and other land.

All of these old settlers were there with their exceeding handsome and graceful California wives, and I could not but remark the singularity of the fact that these rough featured, unrefined and oldish looking men should have been so fortunate as to have been preferred to their handsome California rivals by such young and handsome women as their wives, the belles of the country.

The Mexican architect who planned and laid the adobe of our store got $16 per day in gold, more than our superior judge now receives, and the mud professor who made and toted mud got $5 a day.

So, each adobe in the building cost about $1 and the same money would now build a fine brick building. The lot is now worth $10,000. It cost us $50, and it was the first lot ever sold in this town after the change in things (American occupation).

The sills and rafters came from the pinery on Santa Margarita mountain. The lumber cost $300 per thousand (feet) in San Francisco. After finishing the store, we found nearly all our money was sunk in mud, and we had but little left for stock, but the days of the 50's were lucky days to all. If money was all a person wanted, it would soon turn up.

There were no banks here to discount drafts on San Francisco, no expresses to carry coin, and if one had business with San Francisco, he had to enjoy a lonely mule ride nearly 300 miles to do it. There were no stages or steamers and but seldom a schooner.

Our first district judge was Judge Tefft who had a salary of $500 per month. This had accumulated to $3,000, and he did not know how to collect it without the bother of a land journey. I agreed to collect it if he would give me the use of it for six months with interest, which was then 5% per month.

So, we got our stock, and with it was the first wheelbarrow brought to this county which now plays a little part of this narrative.

We found upon arriving in San Luis Obispo after our trip to San Francisco with stock that the cholera was raging.

The mission was always crowded with Indians, and now they were dying fast and lay putrefying in the old adobe house back of the mission building. The Indian antidote for all ills was a steam bath. They would throw water in a hut over heated rocks and sit in the

The Western part of the TOWN and the MISSION of SAN LUIS OBISPO, 1864. Approach from the Landing

1864— EDWARD VISCHER depicts a group of riders with pack animals following the trail from Mallagh's landing into the San Luis Obispo settlement. The trail at this point eventually became Monterey Street. Among the cluster of buildings would have been the Casa de Wilson, the ruins of the mission's west wall and Casa de Murray.

1875-1934—TO SAVE the deteriorating adobe and rock walls of the mission, a large portion of it was covered with clapboard, and the columns of the portico were eliminated. A New England style wooden belfry was constructed to hold the Peruvian-cast bells.

LOCATED at the back of the mission gardens, this structure served as a kitchen and later, as a stable. Now restored inside, church youth groups use it.

steam. Then, they would run and dive into the cold water of the stream (San Luis Obispo or Stenner Creeks). This helped the cholera to finish them.

We could get no one to handle the dead, but as disasters make heroes, we found one in William Breck, an old mountaineer who came over the mountain with the Bonneville expedition about 1815.

I had brought from San Francisco about 100 cases of the best French cognac, then very cheap, and we made a bargain with Breck. He would haul away the dead Indians in our new wheelbarrow and bury them. We would give him a bottle of cognac for the burial of every Indian.

Breck put a man to digging graves upon the hill where the rocky point is on Morro Street near Buchon. Breck came trotting down the small rise at the corner for us to see the Indian and get his first bottle of cognac.

We got the cognac quick, and we begged him to stop no longer as we did not like dead Indians. And away he went with his corpse in the wheelbarrow, head sticking over the back and legs stuck out in front.

Breck buried eight Indians the first day and kept it up until it was all over. So, old man Breck was San Luis Obispo's first undertaker and the first public hearse was my wheelbarrow.

HIGHLIGHTS IN THE HISTORY OF
MISSION SAN LUIS OBISPO DE TOLOSA

SEPTEMBER 1, 1772- Ground dedicated by Father Junipero Serra for the fifth Franciscan mission in the growing chain in Alta California. Those missions founded before San Luis Obispo were San Diego de Alcala, San Diego, July 16, 1869; San Carlos Borromeo de Carmelo, Carmel, June 3, 1770; San Antonio de Padua, off Jolon Road near Camp Hunter-Leggett, 23 miles southwest of King City, July 14, 1771; and San Gabriel Arcangel, east of Los Angeles, September 8, 1771.

NOVEMBER, 1776- Hostile Indians set fire to the tule thatch roof that covered the first mission building. This led to experimentation in making and using clay roof tiles familiar to the Spanish padres.

DECEMBER 27, 1776- Father Junipero Serra was in San Luis Obispo writing a report on the missions. He may have arrived a few days earlier, spending Christmas day at the mission.

1830- Father Luis Antonio Martinez, who had played such an important role in the development of the mission over a period of 34 years, was banished by Governor Jose Echeandia. Martinez was believed to have given support to a rebel group seeking to overthrow the governor.

1834- Along with other missions in California, San Luis Obispo was secularized.

NOVEMBER, 1842- Padre Jose Miguel Gomez assumed his duties at the mission. He was the first priest ordained in the territory by California's first bishop, Padre Francisco Garcia Diego. The bishop had taken up residence at Mission Santa Barbara a year earlier.

DECEMBER 6, 1846- The mission and its outbuildings with the exception of the church and priest's quarters were sold by the last Mexican governor, Pio Pico, to John Wilson, James Scott and James McKinley for $510. Each of these men already held large Mexican grants.

DECEMBER 14, 1846- Late in the night, struggling against heavy rains, Captain John Fremont and his volunteers occupied the San Luis Obispo settlement for the United States. He made the mission his headquarters during a three-day stay before continuing southward.

AUGUST 20, 1850- The new County of San Luis Obispo rented three rooms in the mission for use as a Court of Sessions, a Records office and jail. The mission served as the county's first courthouse.

SEPTEMBER 2, 1859- The United States Land Commission acted favorably upon a request from Bishop Joseph S. Alemany for the return of the California missions to the Catholic Church.

AUGUST 19, 1872- The mission and the town of San Luis Obispo celebrated the centennial of the dedication of the church. By now, tiles were removed from a portion of the roof and replaced by shingles to relieve the stress of their weight upon the walls.

1875- To preserve the walls of the church, the exterior of most of the building was covered with clapboard. A New England style belfry was constructed to support its Peruvian bells. The balance of the tiles on the roof were removed and replaced by shingles. This was the beginning of the mission's modified "Victorian" architecture.

MARCH 20, 1920- A fire of undetermined cause ignited and destroyed the roof of the church.

1925- Father Daniel Keenan began a drive to restore the mission to its original Spanish-California architecture with the re-establishment in San Luis Obispo of the fiesta of an earlier period. The event was called La Fiesta de las Flores and included a money-making barbecue sponsored by the church.

1934- During Father John Harnett's time at the mission, the 60-year-old clapboard was removed from the side of the church walls. Restoration and reconstruction of the entire building took place. Red tiles again covered the roof, and the church bells were returned to their place in a belfry above the vestibule.

1947- The "ell" of the church, first built in 1893, was extended toward Chorro Street to provide almost as much seating as the nave.

1963- After completion of a new rectory, the priests' quarters in the mission became available for use as a museum.

1970's- The City of San Luis Obispo closed Monterey Street in front of the mission and constructed a plaza which has since become the hub for numerous community events.

ATTERDAG COLLEGE in early years.

FIRST A SCHOOL... THEN SOLVANG

*I*t's little wonder that Solvang became such an attraction for tourists from all over the world. From the beginning, its investors carefully considered every variable important to future Danish settlers. But not even they envisioned their community appealing so widely to so many.

In 1911, a group of Danish educators met in San Francisco to form a corporation for founding a Danish colony. Above all else, they wanted to form a college patterned after the Danish folk school located in Grandview, Iowa and the schools in Denmark.

The West Coast Land Company, well known for land development from Paso Robles in the north to the Santa Ynez Valley, owned 10,000 acres of the old Mexican Rancho San Carlos de Jonata. They sold 9,000 acres of this parcel to the group.

"What had been green pastures strewn with wild flowers and waving grain.." was destined to become a thriving village, Grace Davison wrote in her book, "The Gate of Memories."

True to their plan, Rev. Nordentoft, a member of the original committee, established Atterdag (meaning Other Day) College. The wooden school shown in our postcard was built in 1920. It was privately owned until the Danish Lutheran Church constructed its building in 1921, then it became church property with a Lutheran approved course of study.

The curriculum conformed to that of the Danish folk school located in Nysted, Nebraska and to the schools of Denmark, and it attracted educators, artists and lecturers from all parts of this country as well as the Scandinavian countries.

Mary Harrah, a San Luis Obispo resident, was born in the Santa Ynez Valley. Her grandfather, Nels Nielson (later Nelson) was among the founding members of the colony. She attended Attardag for three summers while growing up during the thirties. Here, she learned the fundamentals of the Lutheran religion as well as the Danish language. Because all Danish folk schools emphasize the concept of a "healthy mind and a healthy body", there was also a substantial sports and physical education program.

"The Danish are very social people," Mary said. "Dania Hall was our center for celebrations."

The Faestelavns Fest, a religious celebration related to Lent, brought days of parties, dances, plays and games. The modern Danish Days conducted in Solvang for tourists is an outgrowth of this folk event, but lacks the meaning and overtones of the original.

Attardag College is gone now, but the large wind chimes of the school were preserved and are enjoyed by the residents of the Solvang Lutheran Home for the aged which is located on the site.

Nowadays, visitors come to see the fairy-tale-like village of Solvang. They try the smorgasbord, the special coffees and the Danish pastries. Many seek out Mission Santa Ines behind the shrubs of the town's south parking lot.

The nearby Alisal Guest Ranch is part of the original Nojoqui Rancho, a 13,522-acre land grant made to Raimundo Carrillo of Santa Barbara during the Mexican period in 1843. One can view a portion of this great rancho from the portico of Mission Santa Ines by looking across the Santa Ynez River.

Solvang is the newest of the towns in the Santa Ynez Valley. Ballard found its beginning in 1860 as a halfway house for the stage run between San Luis Obispo and Santa Barbara. It was established by William N. Ballard, the superintendent of the stagecoach line. Ballard's Station included Ballard's house, a dining room for passengers and a Wells Fargo Express office. Made of adobe, it has been restored and still stands.

Santa Ynez, also located on the stage route, was founded in 1882. It was part of the original 35,499-acre Canada de los Pinos (Canyon of the Pines) grant made to Bishop Garcia Diego for establishing a college to train priests. In the American period, a portion of this grant was bought by Mr. and Mrs. Archibald Hunt. They called their land College Ranch and restored the priest's chapel as their home.

Los Olivos came into existence as the terminus of the Pacific Coast Railroad running from San Luis Obispo and Port Harford.

The Nielsens, the Petersens, the Iversens, the Johnsens, the Christiansens and the other founding families of Solvang have left an extraordinary imprint upon the land where the Chumash Indians once hunted and the cattle of Mission Santa Ines grazed.

HIGHLIGHTS IN THE HISTORY OF
MISSION SANTA INES

SEPTEMBER 17, 1804- Padre Estevan Tapis founds Mission Santa Ines.

DECEMBER 21, 1812- The same earthquake that destroyed Missions Santa Barbara and La Purisima also left the church of Mission Santa Ines in ruins.

1817- A new church was dedicated.

1824- An Indian revolt that began at this mission quickly spread to La Purisima and Santa Barbara missions.

1836- Mission Santa Ines was secularized. Governor Mariano Chico rented the building to Jose Covarrubias for $580 a year. The Indians gradually left the mission.

1843- This mission was returned by the Mexican government to the church. The buildings served as the temporary location for the College of our Lady of Refuge. Soon after, the governor granted the church a rancho for the development of this school for educating priests. It was known as the College Ranch in the American period.

1845- The mission was sold by the Mexican government to Jose Carrillo and the Carrillo family for $7,000.

1862- The United States Land Commission returned the mission buildings to the Catholic Church.

1904- Father Alexander Buckler, a new mission priest, with help from his niece, Mamie Goulet, began a restoration project at the mission that took twenty years to complete.

EARLY PHOTO depicts Mission Santa Ines cemetery where Indians, Spanish, Mexicans and later settlers shared a common burial place. The mission carillon shows in background.

SANTA INES MISSION, LA MISSION DE SANTA INES.

MISSION SANTA INES— Established September 17, 1804 by Padre Estevan Tapis. This building was dedicated in 1817. It is located in the town of Solvang.

REVOLT OF THE CENTRAL COAST CHUMASH MISSION INDIANS

Mission Santa Ines sets high above a grassy canyon fronting north toward pine-forested mountains. Its white-washed adobe walls, red tile roof and spacious multi-columned portico provides such a tranquil aura that it defies the reality of some of the events that occurred there.

For example, there was that time in 1824 when the soldiers of the escolta (the mission guard) set in motion not only a revolt of the Indians associated with that mission but also with the Indian neophytes at Missions Purisima and Santa Barbara.

The trouble began Sunday afternoon, February 21, when Corporal Francisco Cota ordered the flogging of a visiting Indian from Purisima. Though flogging Indians as punishment was practiced at most missions, the Indians witnessing this particular event were somehow enraged beyond reason.

That night, with torches in hand, a group of them lighted fires throughout the mission building and all of its outbuildings, creating an uncontrollable conflagration. Corporal Cota immediately sent for help from the presidio at Santa Barbara. Sergeant Anastacio Carrillo wasted no time in leading a contingent of soldiers to the scene, but upon arrival, received word that the rebels had gone to Purisima Mission.

Meanwhile, at Purisima, the rebels threatened Corporal Tiburcio Tapia and the four or five other soldiers assigned to that Mission. These men quickly gathered their families within the walls of the mission and closed it off. Some four hundred Indians at

Purisima joined the revolt, drawing fire from Tapia's men all night. Finally, the soldiers were out of powder, and they surrendered. Unfortunately, four travelers from Los Angeles arriving during the night were all killed, and the record shows that seven Indians were buried during the next two days after the fray.

The rebel Indians ordered Corporal Tapia and one of the priests, Blas Ordaz, to ride to Santa Ines and tell the Santa Barbara contingent of soldiers to stay away from Purisima or the soldiers of the mission's guard and their families would be killed. But something led the Indians to have second thoughts, and they released their prisoners, sending them to Mission Santa Ines. Padre Antonio Catarino Rodriquez, the second priest at Purisima, remained with the Indian neophytes, and they showed no inclination to harm him.

Now, the Indians controlled Purisima, and they began setting up fortifications, cutting loopholes in the adobe walls of the church and outbuildings to use for firing muskets and shooting arrows. They even mounted two rusty old cannon used in the past for noisemaking during dias de fiesta.

When word of the uprising reached the Indians living at the rancheria next to Mission Santa Barbara, they, too, became

ABOVE: THE LONG PORTICO of Mission Santa Ines looks south to the mountains.

LEFT: TABLES SET for parish luncheon at Mission Ines.

excited. It is said that they began to recall numerous instances of mistreatment by the soldiers. With their fellow Chumash at the other missions taking a stand, they also prepared to rebel.

One day when Padre Antonio Ripoll rode down the hillside to the Santa Barbara presidio, the Indians quickly armed themselves. They demanded that the soldiers assigned to the mission leave, and they promptly shot and wounded two of the guard when they didn't respond.

Presidio Commandante Jose de la Guerra sent a contingent of soldiers to the mission, and they engaged the Indians in fire for several hours. Two Indians were killed and three were wounded. Four soldiers were also wounded before Capt. Guerra pulled his men back to replenish their powder. The Indians used this time to gather up clothing, blankets and food from the mission and then rode into the nearby hills to hide.

Despite objections from the priests, the soldiers returned to the mission and sacked the Indians' adobe abodes and killed a few stragglers. By month's end, twelve victims had been buried at Mission Santa Barbara.

The battle continued to escalate. Now, word reached Governor Luis Arguello at Monterey. He sent 100 men south under command of Lt. Mariano Estrada to help Capt. Guerra fight the rebels. They were to meet at Purisima on a given day. Estrada's company arrived at Purisima ready for a fight. Without waiting for the Santa Barbara company, they opened fire on the adobe walls of the mission with muskets and a four-pounder. The Indians, well protected within the walls, fought back with cannon, muskets and arrows.

Padre Rodriquez finally interceded on behalf of the mission neophytes by walking out into the open to meet with Estrada. His action brought the battle to an end. Sixteen Indians had lost their lives and many were wounded. When Capt. Guerra and his men arrived from Santa Barbara, he and Lt. Estrada condemned seven Indians to be shot. Others were sentenced to 8 and 10 years confinement and work at the presidio.

Rumors of Indian revolt at San Fernando and San Gabriel Missions proved unfounded, but discontent continued among the mission Indians throughout California. Some ran away and joined the inland Tulares, but most were captured by the Mexican army or drifted back to the missions of their own accord. By this time, it was the only life most of them knew.

That February day when the escolta at Mission Santa Ines flogged an Indian, they set in motion the accumulated resentments of Indians all along the mission trail.

TURN-OF-CENTURY— Parishioners wait turn at Mission luncheon.

HIGHLIGHTS IN THE HISTORY OF
MISSION LA PURISIMA CONCEPCION

DECEMBER 8, 1787- Padre Fermin Francisco Lasuen presided over ceremonies in the founding of the mission. Padre Mariano Payeras received assignment here and remained for the next 19 years. During four of those years, he also held the position of el presidente of all of the missions, and Purisima served as the center of mission government.

1804- Mission population reached 1,522.

1810- Mission livestock numbered 10,000 that year.

DECEMBER 21, 1812- The same earthquake destroying Mission Santa Barbara also left Purisma in ruins. The new mission buildings which followed were constructed four miles northeast of the original.

1816-17- A drought occurred. Hundreds of mission sheep died from lack of feed.

1818- Mission Indian houses destroyed by fire.

1823- Padre Payeras dies in service at the mission.

1824- The Indians of this mission as well Missions Santa Ines and Santa Barbara revolt against the harsh treatment of the soldiers.

1833- The year the Mexican Congress decreed that California missions be secularized. Purisima, untended, fell into serious disrepair.

1845- La Purisma and all of its grazing lands were sold by the governor to John Temple in Los Angeles for $1100.

1930's- This mission was never returned to the church.

During the depression years, the California Conservation Corps (CCC] under the national park service began its restoration. When completed it was turned over to the state to be administered as a historic park.

1930— BEFORE RESTORATION began at Mission La Purisma Concepcion.

CALIFORNIA CONSERVATION CORPS worker restoring interior of roof at Mission La Purisima in 1935. It is now administered by the state as a historic park.

1900—IT WOULD be another 35 years before restoration would begin at La Purisma. Most of this portico had collapsed when work started. Today, participating members of CCC can look with pride at their role in re-creating this historical monument.

DATED 1909—Roof tiles were pulling away, columns were cracking. La Purisima would continue deteriorating for many years before its restoration.

LOOKING DOWN to the church sanctuary at La Purisima after restoration. Note plank floor. The original floors would have been first, dirt, then later, adobe or tile.

COLLEGE HOTEL, It was opened in 1889 in expectation of a sudden new influx of travelers.

SANTA YNEZ EXPECTED A BOOM THAT NEVER CAME

*T*he very elegant College Hotel in Santa Ynez was built by the College Land Syndicate in 1888 and 1889 with highest expectations for its success.

But the men who made the decisions for the group made a couple of bad guesses. It was true that the Southern Pacific Railroad had recently constructed track from Soledad south to San Miguel, Paso Robles and Templeton. And certainly, the railroad had built a branch line from Saugus in the South to Santa Barbara. There was every reason to believe the railroad would follow the traditional pattern of the stagecoach line which followed the coast from the north, cut inland to Gaviota, then came into the Santa Ynez Valley through Ballard and Santa Ynez. A good hotel in Santa Ynez looked like a sure-fire investment.

The 30-room hotel opened in 1889. It had an attractive second floor balcony running over a big open porch filled with inviting rocking chairs. With great anticipation, the management waited the day when the hotel's lobby, dining room and all of the guest rooms would be filled with happy guests who had come to enjoy the sunny Santa Ynez Valley.

But the railroad never came. When the north-south connection was finally made in 1901, it completely bypassed Santa Ynez Valley.

The stagecoach continued making regular daily stops at the hotel and some travelers enjoyed its hospitality. People in the Valley enjoyed fine dinners in the hotel's formal dining room, and used it as their social center.

But the stagecoach that came each day with guests for the hotel stopped service in 1901, the year Southern Pacific began offering through service between San Francisco and Los Angeles. Now, the rooms stood vacant most of the time.

On June 8, 1935 at 2 a.m., a fire broke out near a hot water heater and quickly spread throughout the empty building. The hotel and all of its contents were completely destroyed.

HOTEL BRADLEY, SANTA MARIA, CALIFORNIA. 98492

DECEMBER, 1928— The Bradley Hotel and several retail businesses occupied the Southwest corner of Four Corners. A flag pole at the center of Broadway and Main Streets marked the corners of four farms.

FOUR CORNERS IN OLD CENTRAL CITY (SANTA MARIA)

Rudolph Cook tried making a living for his growing family by farming in several different areas in northern California before finally joining a wagon train headed for Los Angeles, and hopefully, better times.

The year was 1869. During a stopover in San Luis Obispo, he heard about recently opened government land available for settlement in the Santa Maria Valley. He quickly found the plot he wanted and made application for it. It was not apparent at the time, but Cook settled at a location that led to a memorable contribution in Central Coast history.

While he and his brother, Larken, built a house, his family lived in the Old Adobe at Guadaloupe with another family. They hauled lumber and materials from Port Harford on a long wagon pulled by an eight-horse team, using the "jerkline" technique common at the time. To control the team, they walked most of the 30 miles over sandy rough terrain.

By fall, they had finished a two-story house and almost immediately, they invited neighbors from miles around to come to a party where they discussed building a school. In February, 1870, the four Cook girls were among the first fifteen pupils to enroll in the Pleasant Valley School.

But life was not easy. They struggled continuously against the sand and dust blown across open fields by strong daily winds. To provide for his family, Cook regularly hunted deer along the river, gathered wild honey, and bartered for other foods and necessities. Until he could dig a well, he hauled water from the Suey Rancho crossing of the Santa Maria River.

Not long after arrival, the Cooks had neighbors. John Thornburgh and his family took over the section of land to the west of them. Then, Isaac Fesler settled the land just north of Thornburgh, and Isaac Miller moved on to the land north of Cook. Each landowner kept informal roads or lanes along the boundary lines where his land touched his neighbors.

At the corner of his land, where it converged with his three neighbors, Thornburgh founded a small cooperative store and postoffice with his neighbor, Cook, and two other men. Each of these men seemed to take a turn as postmaster. Part of the job was to pick up the mail at Suey Crossing. The store was called by several names over the years..the John Thornburgh Company Store, the Farmers' Union and the Grange Store.

Soon after settling his land in 1869, Fesler gave his corner of the land where the four sections came together to Kaiser Brothers, and they, too, built a store. Later, he gave right-of-way land across his property for the track of the Pacific Coast Railroad.

Then Miller also opened a small general store on the corner where his land met with the others. He used much of the rest of his land for a large orchard.

Step-by-step, these men were establishing a community. In 1874, the 'founding fathers' hired an engineer to prepare the plat for a townsite. Each of them donated strips of land for a series of 120-foot-wide streets. They recorded their new townsite in Santa Barbara in 1875, and Central City was officially born.

But then they discovered that too much of their mail was diverted by the postoffice to Central City, Colorado, so in April, 1882, they changed the name of their settlement to Santa Maria. That month, the Pacific Coast Railroad finished track from Port Harford and San Luis Obispo into town and the Santa Maria Times was launched as a weekly newspaper.

Few cities in California have experienced such drastic change. Our 1928 postcard shows Four Corners with its high flag pole designating the converging point of the land belonging to the four founding pioneers. Santa Maria has spread in all directions during the last three decades, and a vast renewal project brought a major shopping mall to the heart of the city as well as several other business centers in other locations.

SANTA MARIA'S early grammar school. Its bell in the tower "called us for the flag salute followed by classes."

Grammar School, Santa Maria, California

SANTA MARIA INN PATIO— The Inn opened May 17, 1917 with 24 bedrooms and a dining room.

SANTA MARIA'S HISTORIC INN

*F*rank McCoy had two special attributes. He derived pleasure from making people comfortable, and he loved beautiful gardens.

Because he admired the style and elegance of English Inns, he made a special study of them. The result was the Santa Maria Inn.

Over the years, McCoy continued to enlarge the Inn. By 1930, it had 85 rooms. He also bought the El Encanto Hotel in Santa Barbara. Both hotels had beautiful gardens.

In recent times, the Inn faced the competition of many large motels, and for a time, it closed completely. Now, under new management, it has enjoyed an exciting revival.

HOUK BUILDING, Santa Maria— John Houk's building housed Santa Maria's early Cadillac agency. Houk served on the board of directors of the First National Bank of Santa Maria.

PYTHIAN CASTLE, SANTA MARIA, CALIFORNIA   OA4300

1930's—THIS BUILDING was referred to as Pythian Castle. It featured Mediteranean style architecture with its tile roof and rail balconies. It was a new concept among Santa Maria's business buildings.

WHITE PAINTED WOODEN CHURCHES with belfries were the style in this country . This Santa Maria structure was highly representative.

NIPOMO RANCH CASA of William Goodwin and Josepha Dana located on a plateau over-looking the 37,000-acre grant made to Dana by Governor Juan Bautista Alvarez in 1837. Dana died in 1858, leaving a wife and thirteen children. After Josepha's death, the Rancho was divided among the children. The eldest child, John, assumed responsibility for sale of a portion of the land as is exhibited in this postcard mailing piece he used. See the article Narrow Gauge Rails Across the Ranchos at the back of the book for information about the breakup of this grant.

Return in 10 days to

JOHN F. DANA,

NIPOMO, San Luis Obispo Co., Cal.

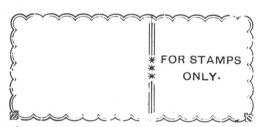

FOR STAMPS
ONLY.

This valley is destined to be one of the finest fruit sections of San Luis Obispo County. For agriculture and cattle raising this valley is not excelled. Another fact that has been demonstrated is that this county is not excelled in the State for butter and cheese. Great inducements are offered to intending immigrants from the fact that no irrigation is required. By thorough cultivation the moisture is abundant to produce the crops. For fruit raising this section has passed the experimental station. There have already been set out over one hundred thousand trees and as many more are in contemplation. Water is abundant in all parts of the valley. We have a good market for our produce in San Francisco to the north and Los Angeles to the south. The produce shipped from Nipomo Depot for the year ending December 1, 1893, were as follows: Barley, 30,215 sacks; Wheat, 12,415 sacks; Oats, 11,632; Rye, 1,0.3 sacks; Beans, 29,935 sacks; this includes only what has been shipped, about two-thirds of the crop harvested; Mustard, 150 sacks; of Potatoes there will be at least 10,000 sacks. Nipomo is on the line of the Pacific Coast Railway, 22 miles south of San Luis Obispo, the county seat. The Southern Pacific Railroad is now being completed. This will give us a through line to all Eastern cities, when tourists and home seekers can ride direct from any point East of the Rockies through our great valley over one of the most beautiful scenic routes on the Coast. The town of Nipomo is conveniently located in the center of the great Nipomo valley. It contains the usual variety of business houses, churches, schools, express and telegraph companies. We have an excellent system of water works which furnishes an abundant supply of pure, spring water. There is no section in the State that offers greater inducements to the homeseeker of moderate means than Nipomo. Send for circulars.

Newsom's Arroyo Grande Warm Springs.

SAN LUIS OBISPO COUNTY, CALIFORNIA.

Located in the Hills 2 1-2 Miles From Arroyo Grande and 5 Miles From Oceano, the Southern Pacific Rail Road Station and 6 Miles From the Beach

◆·◎▷ ◆ A MOST PERFECT WINTER RESORT ◆ ▷◎·◆

HAVING A WARM TEMPERATURE THE YEAR ROUND

The Waters of the Several Springs are a specific for piles, rheumatism, nasal catarrh, neuralgia, liver and kidney complaints, scrofula, diseases of the stomach, dropsy, female complaints, etc..

━━━ Analysis of the Water of Newsom's Warm Springs ━━━

DR. WINSLOW ANDERSON, ANALYSIST.

Temperature. 100.5° F., U. S. Gal. contains Grains		U. S. Gal. contains Grains	
Sodium Chloride	4.10	Calcium Carbonate	8.25
Sodium Carbonate	1.75	Calcium Sulphate	.75
Sodium Sulphate	3.92	Ferrous Carbonate	3.99
Potassium Carbonate	.15	Alumina	.33
Potassium Sulphate	2.90	Silica	2.03
Magnesium Carbonate	6.41	Organic Matter	.27
Magnesium Sulphate	2.47		
Total			37.32

FREE CAMPING **NO SALOON**

Free Carbonic Anhydride 1490 cubic inches free Sulphated Hydrogen, 356 cubic inches

El Pizmo, Oceano and La Grande Beaches which afford the best drives in the State, and where clamming and fishing are always in order, is within easy drive of the springs. No summer, no winter--spring and fall being the only seasons. Cottages to let for light housekeeping. Family board. Single meals 25 cents. Baths 25 cents. Telephone Suburban 75.

MRS. ANNA NEWSOM, Proprietor.

(c. 1902)

A FIVE MILE BUGGY ride from the new town of Oceano brought Southern Pacific Railroad passengers to Newsom's Springs for the baths.

HOT SPRINGS CURE ALWAYS IN VOGUE

One of the historical messages we get from our collection of old central coast postcards is the enduring attraction of hot springs resorts. The advertising postcard shown here was prepared to woo customers to Newsom's Arroyo Grande Warm Springs after the Southern Pacific Railroad reached the new nearby community of Oceano in 1895.

In 1876 during the annual Fourth of July celebration marking the nation's centennial year, David Newsom gave a lecture sketching the history and current status of life in that area. Among many other worthy developments, he mentioned his own Newsom's White Sulphur Springs, later called Newsom's Arroyo Grande Warm Springs, situated in a tranquil glen about two miles southeast of the Arroyo Grande settlement.

"The amount of water from these springs is sufficient to bathe several hundred persons daily," he told his audience. The water contained large quantities of sulphur, iron and magnesium, and it bubbled out of the ground at about 100 degrees Fahrenheit. At the time, a large garden, orchard and vineyard helped make the place attractive.

Seventeen years later, a roving reporter named A. S. Austen visited Newsom's Springs. He found the place "peculiarly lovely and romantic." He mentioned catching the strong smell of sulphur even while approaching the place along the wagon road through the gulch.

At the time, he found Newsom building new bath houses and constructing a "curbing around the spring." There were eight furnished cottages for rent to tourists at prices ranging from 15 to 30 dollars a month. During those years before medicine had developed into a precise science, the hot springs not only attracted people who came for a vacation but others seeking cures for all sorts of ailments.

The late Dorothy Bilodeau once said that her father, Judge E. P. Unangst of San Luis Obispo, occasionally rented a cabin at Newsom's and took the whole family. They sometimes spent a full month during the summer. Newsom's property included several hundred acres around the springs, and the children had the time of their lives running free in the orchard and hills, swimming and picnicking.

Newsom's Springs disappeared long ago, but others in Southern San Luis Obispo County filled the gap. An example is Sycamore Mineral Springs. It is on the road to Avila Beach. These springs are mentioned in the old Tribune as early as 1892. We are told that these hot waters first rushed to the surface at sometime during the 1890's while

men were drilling for oil. They didn't find oil, but they discovered the product for a new enterprise. By the Twenties, this resort was well developed with many cabins, bathhouses and massage rooms.

Some groups made day-long excursions aboard the little Pacific Coast Railway which stopped at the springs coming and going between Avila Beach and San Luis Obispo.

During the late Sixties and early Seventies, hot springs enjoyed a revival with a special interest among young people discovering all things "natural."

It seems as though aficionados of hot springs make such places a special world of their own. They claim curing qualities in the mineral waters as they sink back into their steaming tubs, sip their wine and luxuriate in hedonistic glee.

MAIN STREET   ARROYO GRANDE CAL

POST MARKED JULY 10, 1908— "This is the main street," the writer told her friend. "You can imagine what the others are like." Mission San Luis Obispo had produce gardens here almost from its beginning.

*SINCE EARLY in this century, Arroyo Grande has enjoyed its swinging
bridge across the "Arroyo Grande." It has gone through numerous repairs
and restorations. Most of the "swing" has been eliminated for safety reasons.*

*THE SMALL RIVER through the community of Arroyo Grande was not always as well-controlled as
it has been since the construction of Lopez Dam. During the winter of 1914, the river overflowed,
destroying a section of Branch Street, the principle thoroughfare.*

c1910-EARLY DUNE BUGGY?- This personalized postcard shows the late Hazel and Grant Hansen with a friend on the beach at Pismo. Their white horse came with the general store they bought and operated in Avila. In the background, one of the blue-striped platform tents of Tent City.

TENT CITY ON THE BEACH IN OLD EL PISMO

*T*ravelers who know first-hand the weariness of jet lag, the discomfort of "tourista" or the blur of the landscape seen from some of the world's super trains may take inspiration from this early picture postcard tour of El Pizmo, California at the turn-of-the-century.

"For twenty miles the broad beach extends as level as the sea and as smooth as a floor washed by the ever coming and receding waves...the sand hardened by the beating of the water so the tracks of horses and wagons scarcely leave an imprint."

That's the way Editor Myron Angel saw this South County beach one day in 1885

when he left the newspaper office, rented a buggy and a team of fine trotting horses at Crawford Livery Stable in San Luis Obispo and followed the wagon road to this developing seaside settlement.

For miles and miles, Angel witnessed tourists in their buggies silently rolling along the long white stretch of beach scarcely "conscious of the movemnt, so enraptured with the spell of the experience." Campers arrived in covered wagons with sleek horses or fine mules and made campsites among the dunes and in the groves of trees above the beach.

Editor Angel paid fifty cents for a fine

lunch at the Pizmo Hotel and sold an advertisement to the manager, M. Meherin.

"The Pismo and our grand bay will become the favorite resort of the Pacific Coast," Angel predicted.

Jean Hubbard, writer and collector of South County history, reminds us that this rising beach community and all of the land around it was part of the early Mexican land grant known as El Pizmo. It belonged to John Price and his descendants, including the Pizmo Hotel.

Soon after P.C. Dolliver assumed management of the hotel in 1887, he announced his association with Messrs. A. E. Pomeroy and Charles W. Stinson, well known "managers and manipulators of the celebrated Long Beach property near Wilmington." Dolliver and his associates planned to offer "villa" properties close to the beach. These coastal lots sold for $150 to $500. Buyers paid one third down, one third after six months and the balance due at the end of one year.

But for people wanting only a pleasant vacation at the beach, another type of facility became available at Pizmo shortly before the turn of the century. It was known as Tent City. This kind of accommodation sprang up along the beaches of California all of the way to Coronado.

At Pizmo, units were constructed of blue and white striped canvas stretched over 14' x 18' wooden frames on pine-covered platforms. Each tent had a small porch. Inside, curtains separated the space into two bedrooms, a living area and a buffet kitchen. The $8 weekly rent included beds, linen, gas stoves and dishes.

The late Ruth Paulding, a lifelong resident of Arroyo Grande, recalled with

c1910-TENT CITY, PISMO BEACH- Taken from a captive balloon, this photo shows that more than 100 tents made up old Tent City. In the foreground, the Wave Hotel. The building with the barrel roof was the Pavilion where a variety of entertainments were offered visitors. The stretch of land beyond the tents encompasses the present-day Shell Beach and Pacific Palisades.

"Watching the Bathers"   PISMO BEACH, CAL.

"Dear Madge, It's a warm day on the beach. Glad to escape the Valley heat for a few days. We'll stay for a week. Going to try the hotel dinner tonight."

pleasure staying at Tent City with a girl-friend. Accounts vary as to how long Tent City existed, but in a Harvest Festival issue of the old Arroyo Grande Herald, Dorothy Godfrey, a local resident, said that she had rented a tent at the beach as late as 1937. Although such easy-going times have long since disappeared, Editor Angel's prediction about Pizmo Beach becoming a "favorite resort" has come to pass. Fine resort-style motels now line the beach of that old Mexican land grant.

With the years, the name of the community has changed at least three times. At first, it was El Pizmo, then Pismo and finally, Pismo Beach.

PADDLEWHEEL STEAMER SANTA MARIA—During the 1880's, this steamer docked at Pismo Wharf to take loads of bituminous rock hauled from Edna Valley.

CAMPERS WITH TENTS, HORSES AND BUGGIES provide us a view of turn-of-century beach vacations at old El Pismo. It is Sunday. Women in billowing long dresses and umbrellas stroll with husbands in dark suits after church services. Reproduced by The Photique, Pismo Beach.

JULY 4,1894— Taken from a postcard signed by B. Leedham and enlarged by the Photique in Pismo Beach. This photo shows a wooden Ferris wheel, tents on the beach, horses and buggies and visitors in festive dress.

c1928—PRICE STREET, PISMO BEACH— At the time, Price Street was also the El Camino Real. The early wooden garage is gone, but the brick hotel remains in 1989. Reproduced by The Photique, Pismo Beach.

THE PISMO INN— Located on the high bank above the beach, this inn owned by Irene Carpenter was predecessor to the many resort motels that line the bluff north of Pismo Beach. It's lounge with rock fireplace and wood paneled walls gave it a seaside lodge appearance.

STILL ANOTHER VIEW of old Tent City in Pismo.

El Pizmo Beach, near San Luis Obispo, Cal.

THE BLUFFS above early Pismo Beach made good farmland and stood vacant for decades after settlement. Eventually, subdivisions of small homes at Shell Beach and then large resort motels filled the land.

Dance Pavillion, Pismo Beach Cal.

THIS EARLY PAVILION served as center for every celebration... Fourth of July programs, dances, lectures and band concerts. Here, a 1920's crowd gathers for a social event.

POSTMARKED AVILA 1909— This complete oil processing plant was located where the present-day Pacific Palisades subdivision developed some years after World War II. "Dear Little Mother," the message read, "I am too busy to write a letter, but will do so soon."

1228 Oil fields, seven miles from San Luis Obispo, California.

DATED 1910– These derricks were located in the Edna area in the same location where some oil is still pumped today.

FIRST PRESBYTERIAN CHURCH , San Luis Obispo— Built in 1905 using rock quarried from Bishop Mountain.

A 19ᵗʰ CENTURY MAN AND HIS CHURCH

T hose chimes that ring out each day at noon from the San Luis Obispo First Presbyterian Church to warm the hearts of all who hear them are actually on tape. Although McDowell Reid Venable would undoubtedly approve of the idea, he'd surely be astounded if he were still around.

But he'd be pleased to know how the church turned out. It took a quarter century after California gained statehood for enough people living in San Luis Obispo to decide to build a Presbyterian Church. It was Venable who prodded it into existence. Young Venable and his very supportive wife, Alice, arrived in San Jose from Virginia in 1868, then made their way by stagecoach to San Luis Obispo where they settled and contributed to the community all the rest of their lives.

He was somewhat a rarity at that time in San Luis Obispo because he had a college education, and he had served in the Civil War. As a Southerner, he saw action in the Confederate Army and participated in several major battles including the second battle of Manas-

sas at Antietam where he was wounded and reported dead. Toward the end of the war, he served as acting captain of engineers in charge of placing pontoon bridges.

Soon after arriving in town, the Venables joined the Episcopal Church, the only protestant place of worship available. Although he served as Episcopalian junior warden, he and Alice continued to lean toward Presbyterianism.

The very next year, 1869, a second protestant church organized. The Methodists began meeting in an unfinished building placed in a temporary location. When the Catholic Mission Church started selling lots in the old mission garden along present-day Garden Street between Higuera and Marsh Streets, the Methodists bought a lot and moved their building to that location. Their place of worship became known as the Garden Street Church, attracting people of many protestant denominations.

In 1872, Venable was elected County Judge, a position he held until 1880. Mean-

First Presbyterian Church of San Luis Obispo, California
Founded 1875

time, in July 1874, a Reverend Thomas Fraser, a missionary agent of the Synod of the Pacific, came to town hoping to gather Presbyterians into the fold. During his visit, he conducted the first Presbyterian service in the community. At Judge Venable's urging, the Reverend returned again some months later. By this time, Venable had rounded up nine other people besides himself and his wife, and they became the charter members of San Luis Obispo's First Presbyterian Church. Judge Venable was elected ruling elder, and kept the Session records until the year of his death in 1907.

Venable led a very full life in the community. He was delegate to the national Democratic Convention at Baltimore the year that Horace Greeley was nominated for president of the United States. In 1886, he served in the California legislature. Later, he was president of the San Luis Obispo Board of Trade, the forerunner to the Chamber of Commerce. He was also one of the organizers of the San Luis Obispo Commercial Bank. He became president of the bank in 1893. As the Southern Pacific Railroad, now laying rails across the Cuesta grade, neared town, he helped form the San Luis Obispo Investment and Development Company.

The Presbyterians held services in the Methodist Church for a long time. After five years, there were still only 24 members, but they started building a small wooden church on the southeast corner of Morro and Marsh Streets.

During 1883-84, the next church building was constructed. It would accommodate 200 people and had a belfry and bell over the vestibule for calling people to service. But the belfry proved dangerous in high winds, actually shaking the whole building, so it was removed. The congregation continued to grow, and they bought more land along Marsh Street.

The Presbyterians built their third church after the turn-of-the-century. The original little wooden building was moved from its corner location to make room for the stone building which exists today. The stone was quarried from Bishop Mountain, and the new building was dedicated in 1905. The Hart building, alongside the present-day church on Marsh, was constructed in 1929 and named for Reverend Frederick Hart, the pastor at the time.

The First Presbyterian Church celebrated its centennial in 1975, and since that date, a new fellowship hall has been added.

The ghosts of McDowell and Alice Venable and the other nine charter members of the congregation must sometimes take a corner pew in the back of the sanctuary during services and smile at what they wrought. The church now has 650 members.

MORRO ROCK and the sandspit in an earlier time.

MORRO BAY... ITS ROOTS AS A COMMUNITY

Standing on the gently sloping land,
That rises back from Morro's shining bay,
I look along the shining stretch of strand,
And hear the roar of surf, and see the spray...
— C. Elwoods

The local nineteenth century poet who wrote the above words about Morro Bay and its famous rock was perhaps better attuned to the feelings of present-day visitors and residents of the community than its original settlers. Early businessmen saw Morro Bay as a commercial port and a place to make money.

In 1877, Domingo Pujol, owner of the Mexican land grant named Moro y Cayucos finally succeeded in clearing title to his land through the Supreme Court of California. Before that time, he had sold some parcels with clouded titles, including a 160-acre piece to Franklin Riley. It was Riley's land that became the City of Morro Bay. In 1870, Riley formed a partnership with a Captain Williams who owned the Schooner Alexina. They built a small wharf, and began buying, selling and transporting merchandise between Morro Bay and San Francisco.

In 1872, Ezra Stocking opened the first general store and became postmaster. In 1873, Morro took an accounting of itself. It had fourteen houses, two general stores, two blacksmith shops, a shoemaker, a carpenter shop and a butcher shop. The new settlement also had a second and sturdier wharf with a warehouse. The Steamer Coquille touched regularly and several schooners came into the bay soliciting freight business.

After Pujol cleared title to his rancho, he subdivided the land into small farms. Crops and dairy products of the new land-owners soon increased business at the port. Two men, acting as agents for a Santa Cruz firm set up the Morro Bay Lumber Company.

The new century arrived before businessmen saw opportunities in promoting tourism.

CAYUCOS BEACH AND WHARF, 1907— These fashionable bathers are (l. to r.) Meda Biaggini; Jean Trout, a Cal Poly student and friend of the Biaggini girls; Mrs. Henry Cass, daughter-in-law of Captain Cass; Esther Biaggini and Laura Biaggini. The Biaggini girls were sisters of Mary Biaggini Hartzell who provided these cards and pictures. The building on the wharf housed a tractor used for pile driving. In later years, an abalone cannery operated on the wharf.

IN OLD CAYUCOS...RIGHT MAN, RIGHT TIME, RIGHT PLACE

*T*ake a long sandy beach next to a body of water such as Estero Bay, an inlet off the California central coast.

Make sure this beach and bay is reasonably well-cradled against winds and high tides, ideally located on the leeward side of a protective shoulder of land like Point Estero.

Now, add a man of the sea, a strong young sailor with a turn-of-mind like that of James Cass.

Bring these elements together, and you have the potential for an old-fashioned 19th century landing place that will accommodate trading ships plying the waters of the Pacific Coast.

Finally, call in a local land promoter like Chauncy Hatch Phillips. He will subdivide the area into town lots. The result will be the beginning of a port and beach settlement like Cayucos.

The ladies in the first picture postcard accompanying this article exhibit the daring swimwear fashions in vogue at Cayucos in

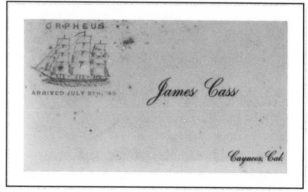

JAMES CASS' BUSINESS CARD—It informs its recipient that Cass arrived on the three-masted, square-rigged Brig Orpheas in 1849.

1907. How carefree and uninhibited they obviously feel without their usual ankle-length dresses and high-button shoes. Neither slacks nor shorts were known by girls of their day. In the background, we see the wharf that berthed so many early trading ships.

We are told that Cass, later referred to as Capt. Cass by people of the area, came to the Central Coast in about 1867 hoping to become a farmer, but he was too much a man of the sea. He soon established a lightering service, transporting goods in small boats to and from coastal steamers that anchored in Estero Bay. The work was extremely precarious. There were times when the sea was so rough that he lost everything loaded on his surfboat.

But he progressed. Within a few years he formed a partnership with a Capt. Ingalls. With this financial support, he built a 380-foot-long wharf, a small store and a warehouse. Across the wagon road from the wharf he constructed a two-story house for his family and himself. The old house still stands, now vacant, weather-beaten and without much hope of preservation.

In 1874, Capt. Cass gathered more partners...William Beebee, John Hanford and L. Schwartz, three county entreprenuers...and they formed a business called J. Cass & Co. They extended the wharf into deeper water, improved warehouse facilities and added a horse-drawn railway for moving goods between docked ships and the warehouse.

Now, larger vessels could dock alongside the wharf, a real boon for farmers seeking more lucrative markets for their products.

Mary Biaggini Hartzell, a lifelong resident of Cayucos, still fondly refers to Capt. Cass as Papa Cass, and recalls that the wharf was used as an abalone cannery beginning in the early years of the century.

REMNANT of early Moro y Cayucos Mexican land grant, this adobe house eventually collapsed. It was located across from the present-day Cayucos grammer school just off Highway 1.

A DRAMATIC sketch of Cayucos Landing where steamers received and disembarked both freight and passengers during the late 19th century.

BANK OF CAYUCOS—By 1893, Cayucos enjoyed a full complement of retail establishments. However, a fire the night of September 8, 1893 destroyed nearly all of the business buildings along the main street including this bank, the Cosmopolitan Hotel, the Commercial Bank, a couple of saloons, the Odd Fellows Hall, two general stores, a drug store, a barber shop, and a stable. The landing on the opposite side of the wide street was saved.

A six-horse team pulling two high rack wagons along the street in old Cayucos.

YOUNG HENRY K. CASS, son of James Cass, with friend in horseless carriage at beginning of the century. The woman's duster and neckerchief protect her from neck to ankles against dust of the road. With her scarf tucked tightly under hat, she arrived at the party almost clean.

c1906-07— HENRY and MARGE (SANDERS) CASS on road above Cayucos. Wharf and warehouse show in background.

MARGE (SANDERS) CASS and friend test classy new coupe.

BELOW: DURING the thirties an abalone cannery operated on Cayucos wharf. Here, two vessels are anchored. Horse-drawn flat cars pulled catch to wharf cannery.

STEAMSHIP ORIZABA— Made regular stops at Santa Barbara, Port Harford (now Port San Luis), Cayucos, and occasionally at San Simeon on the Central Coast. Operated by Pacific Coast Steamship Company.

CUESTA GRADE- c1914- Still used by horse and wagon travelers, the Cuesta Grade in the Santa Lucia Mountains provided a real adventure for early automobile drivers.

BUILDING A PART OF THE KING'S HIGHWAY

How a portion of the mission and stage-coach trail gave way to the automobile...

For several days in December, 1891, heavy rains soaked the Cuesta road, creating deep mud and a dangerously slippery downgrade south toward San Luis Obispo. In spite of conditions, two stage-coaches left Santa Margarita at the same time one evening, both loaded with passengers.

As the first coach descended the grade in the dark, driver Jim Myer knew the gait of the team was too fast, but neither tightening the reins nor pulling on the wagon brakes slowed the alarming speed. The horses, pushed by the weight of the stagecoach, panicked. At one particularly precarious turn, the coach flipped, spilling passengers, baggage and freight. Luckily, Frank Smith, the second driver, successfully crowded everyone aboard his coach for the ride into San Luis Obispo. Dr. Nichols bandaged the wounded and all passengers were safely bedded down in the new Ramona Hotel.

Such accidents were all too common. As far back as 1850, the County Court of Sessions had tried to make the Cuesta safer by allotting $1000 to improve it. Persistent horsemen, wagoners and cattle drovers swore their determination, ate its dirt and gradually shaped its ruts into a precarious route. Then in 1876, the County raised $20,000 through the sale of bonds to build a real dirt wagon road. This road, "though steep and narrow, is still

1922- The two-lane dirt road over the Cuesta constructed in 1914 was allowed to settle for 6 1/2 years before paving began. Here, an early loader lifts rock into a dump truck.

ESTRADA GARDENS— At the foot of the Cuesta during Swiss-Italian celebration. The horse and buggy still served as principal transportation, but the automobile was making small inroads along the Central Coast.

CUESTA ROAD during those serene years when a portion of it followed the canyon base rather than the side of the mountains.

traversable on the southern ascent where it winds along the westerly slope of San Luis Obispo canyon," Lester Gibson, district engineer, wrote back in 1938. Still, during all of the years of its use, old newspapers reported stagecoach and wagon accidents along its route.

In 1914, we find that the state let a contract for a new road to be built down the eastside of the Cuesta with only a 6-1/2 percent grade. After construction, they let it settle for seven years before paving. In 1922, for the first time, "a contract was awarded for paving, reshaping the road's surface, super-elevating the curves and daylighting shape points."

The new 20-foot-wide road had two lanes with reinforced concrete curbs. As one of our old picture postcards show, it did not include a shoulder nor a divider strip, but it represented "a fine example of mountain highway construction," according to a 1924 issue of California Highways magazine. By the early twenties, average Americans could afford Henry Ford's new assembly-line built Model-T, and horse-and-buggy transportation was soon displaced in most of the country.

In 1938, Gibson announced that "Modern engineering skill at last has conquered Cuesta Pass.." He made this statement after completion of a new four-lane highway on the grade.

The new Cuesta was officially opened and dedicated before a large crowd by Governor Frank Merriam on Saturday, November 5, 1938. San Luis Obispo Mayor L. F. Sinsheimer, County Supervisors Board Chairman T. Arnold and San Luis Obispo Chamber of Commerce President Cecil Evans gave welcoming talks.

The governor cut a handmade riata

EARLY CUESTA ROAD through canyon.

stretched across the highway with a machete borrowed from the mission as part of the dedication ceremony. At last, all felt, the major barrier to safety along the coastal highway had been overcome.

But present-day Cal Trans Maintenance Engineer Herbert Filipponi, a native San Luis Obispan, reminds us that the highway continued through San Luis Obispo city streets as part of its route. From the north, travelers arrived in town on Monterey Street at the point where the Motel Inn is still located. Travelers then turned south at Santa Rosa Street and west again on Marsh. For some years, the highway continued out pres-

ent-day lower Higuera Street. Later, the interchange at the end of Marsh Street was built.

Construction to bypass the city occurred between 1953-56. Some years later, Cal Trans proposed a complete new Cuesta highway alignment along the ridge of the Santa Lucias, but a massive public outcry to preserve the mountain tops led to withdrawal of this plan. Since 1968, many curves have been eliminated or modified, the roadbed widened and dividers placed. However, deep concerns about the long-run safety of the Cuesta probably remain as prevalent today as they did during horse-and-buggy days.

 Maintenance Yard San Luis Obispo

BEFORE 1930— The Central Coast Highway Division office was located next to the Southern Pacific Railroad roundhouse in San Luis Obispo. The roundhouse was taken down in 1959-60.

JANUARY 1, 1930— Developing new site of Central Coast Highway Division Offices and shops. They were located on lower Higuera Street, San Luis Obispo.

JANUARY, 1914— A dump truck and teams of horses with plows exhibit "state of the art" equipment in road building.

JANUARY, 1914— Men hand-shoveled concrete into wheel barrows for pouring culverts and edging along portions of the Cuesta.

JANUARY, 1914— Workers using wheelbarrows with metal-rimmed wheels work in a relay from concrete mixer and gravel pile to a road area needing fill.

1914— CENTRAL COAST Highway Division trucking equipment used on the Cuesta grade.

1913— RESIDENT Engineer's Office Wagon.

TEAMS AND equipment for grading roads.

1922—New two-lane 20-foot highway on the east side of the canyon with concrete curb but without a shoulder.

FEBRUARY, 1930— Highway 101 entered San Luis Obispo on Monterey Street. The structure on the right, now called Motel Inn, shows a sign that reads only Motel. It was the first business in the country offering accommodations for travelers to use the now popular term, Motel. It opened for business in 1926.

1938— BRIDGE ACROSS Southern Pacific Railroad tracks through the Cuesta.

1938— SAME BRIDGE shown at top of page after completion.

OCTOBER, 1934— This scene shows arched electric sign. During these years, lower Higuera in San Luis Obispo was still Highway 101. The sign was paid for by the Monday Club, a dynamic women's group started during the mid- 1920's. The Highway Division office is located on the left.

SATURDAY, November 5, 1938— New four-lane highway across the Cuesta grade completed. Here, Governor Frank Merriam and local notables participate in dedication ceremonies. Girls in swim suits promote Morro Bay. Gov. Merriam cut riata opening the highway.

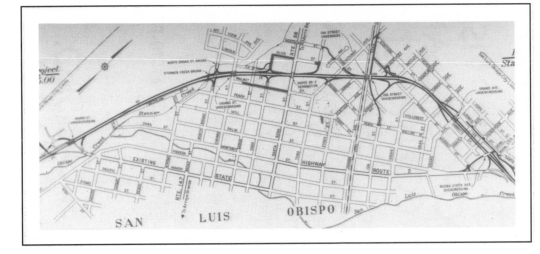

1953-56— HIGHWAY WORK began to bypass San Luis Obispo. Map shows proposed route and off ramps. The city lost many through streets in the process.

Rodeo at Santa Margarita Ranch near San Luis Obispo, Cal. May 3, 08

SANTA MARGARITA RANCHO— Neighbors gathered May 3, 1908 to brand cattle, enjoy a barbecue and compete in riding, roping and other contests.

PASTORAL SANTA MARGARITA RANCHO

There is something warm and even comfortable in the pastoral scene and the name of the great Santa Margarita Rancho. As one views the rancho to the east after leaving the Cuesta grade and passing the off ramp that leads to the main street of the community of the same name, the headquarters of the rancho in the distance comes into view. Who would guess that such a peaceful spot has been the site for so many momentous historical events.

Our picture postcard depicts cowboys preparing for a round-up on the rancho May 3, 1908. It is reminiscent of even earlier times when neighboring ranchos without fences came together to identify, separate and brand their cattle.

Santa Margarita Rancho was the most northern of a group of ranchos operated by the padres and Indian neophytes of Mission San Luis Obispo. In 1775, the Indians constructed a large rock-walled building in the center of their thatched roof and adobe rancheria. The structure served as their place of worship, a mission assistencia. Here, visiting priests from the mission conducted mass and all of the other services of the church. In this building, hundreds of Indian children received baptism, young couples took vows of matrimony and Indians who died received last rites. If any major construction should occur in this area, builders should be prepared to allow an archeological dig. Somewhere nearby there must be a deeply buried

Indian cemetery and the remains of a village containing a rich body of knowledge that merges catholicism and Indian culture. Today, a modern roof covers the old rock wall and the building conveniently provides farm storage.

After the Mexican government confiscated mission lands in 1833, this building, like other mission properties, fell into disrepair. Joaquin Estrada, only 24 years old at the time, petitioned for and was granted the 17,735-acre rancho from Mexican Governor Pro Tem Manuel Jimeno on September 27, 1841. In his petition, he pointed out that the mission no longer used the land, and he promised to respect the acreage used for planting by a group of Indians who remained on the rancho.

The location of the rancho along the mission trail became a regular stopping place for travelers in California. Mexican Governor Pio Pico and General Jose Castro met at the ranch to plan strategy after the American takeover at Monterey, Yerba Buena (San Francisco) and Sonoma. In December, 1846, Captain John Fremont executed an Indian on the rancho because he carried a message from Jose Jesus Pico, the justice of the peace at the Mission San Luis Obispo settlement. He also arrested Estrada, Inocente Garcia and Jose Mariano Bonilla. They were released when they volunteered their services to the Captain.

Tales of high living by Estrada are told and retold. Fellow ranchers and families gathered from miles around to enjoy weeklong rodeos, barbecues, horse racing and rollicking fiestas. Estrada dissipated much of his easily gained wealth.

In April, 1861, the date the Santa

SANTA MARGARITA RANCH HOUSE— This house served many tenants including its owner, State Senator Patrick Murphy, during the later years of the 19ᵗʰ century.

ABOVE: RUINS of Mission Assistencia on the Santa Margarita Rancho before a modern barn was built over it.

LEFT: GATE to Santa Margarita Rancho from the town of Santa Margarita.

Margarita was finally patented by the United States Land Commission, title company records show ownership passing to Martin and Mary Murphy of San Jose. Within a few years, Murphy also purchased the nearby Asuncion and Atascadero Ranchos.

After graduation from Santa Clara College, their son, Patrick, took charge of his parent's property, a total of nearly 70,000 acres in various parts of California. Patrick was viewed by local people as a jovial, fun-loving Irishman. He served in the California Assembly and was elected state senator three times.

Like Estrada, Murphy also entertained lavishly. When the new town of Santa Margarita was laid out on his rancho in February, 1889, Murphy announced a "Grand Barbecue" prepared by him and his vaqueros. Half of California must have heard about it. There was almost a traffic jam of wagon teams along the Cuesta road. People from the north arrived by train to see the new terminus for the Southern Pacific Railroad in this part of the territory. One day the line would continue all of the way to Los Angeles. Two thousand people found their way to this outing and the land auction that accompanied it.

"If there is one thing more than another that General Murphy knows all about, it is managing an old-fashioned barbecue to a tee-y-te," Tribune Editor Benjamin Brooks reported to his readers.

They sold 102 lots in the new town that day. Now, developers are again trying to persuade the county to allow further subdivision of this great Mexican land grant. Whatever occurs, we should work to save our mission assistencia and a good spread of land immediately around it. Somehow, it seems right to honor the Indians who build it and to maintain it as a traveler's haven.

Atascadero California, "The Beautiful"

1920— ATASCADERO ADMINISTRATION BUILDING with La Plaza Inn at the far left. When Southern California newspaper editors gathered in the community that year, every car in the vicinity was called into use to tour them throughout the county.

ATASCADERO'S EARLY INDOOR SHOPPING CENTER

Not all of the business spaces were rented, and there was still some touching up to do in Atascadero's new mercantile building when January 20, 1917 rolled around. But no one saw any reason to wait longer to celebrate the completion of the structure that would house the community's indoor shopping center.

Its completion signaled another victory for E. G. Lewis, the founder and visionary for the creation of a fine community.

Atascadero Colony already had a domed administration building for conducting governmental affairs as well as a sizeable "printery" building with presses and equipment for the production of a newspaper, a magazine and a host of brochures and broadsheets used to attract settlers and land buyers.

Lewis told residents that the new building would soon house many small retail stores within one larger store. As a group, these businesses would meet all of a family's ordinary shopping needs...groceries, drugs, clothing, hardware.

The top floor would serve as the community's hostelry, and it would be called La Plaza Inn.

The Atascadero News reported some 800 people from the community and surrounding area crowded the new building that day. They wandered through the spacious structure imagining shelves and counters filled with colorful goods of all kinds and undoubtedly marveled at the accomplishments of their community's founder. The evening turned to magic for them when the band began to play, refreshments were served and people were invited to dance on both the main floor and the mezzanine.

The "housewarming" was only the beginning of celebrations in this building, according to Marguerite Travis, author of the small book titled "The Birth of Atascadero."

On March 4, the grand opening of the businesses led to a long-remembered buying spree by both residents and people from surrounding communities. On July 4, 1917, Governor William E. Stephens delivered his Independence Day speech from a grandstand constructed in front of the building. During its years, the inn served as a center for a variety of conferences, including one held by the Southern California newspaper editors in 1920.

Most oldtimers in Atascadero will tell you that Lewis had a good thing going, but he seemed unable to contain his visions and investments within realistic bounds. The inn and mercantile building came under management of Fred Bartholomew in 1926 after Lewis filed for bankruptcy. Everything that Lewis owned was taken by creditors.

Maizie Adams, a longtime resident and ardent student of the history of Atascadero, shared her notes with this writer. They show many good times and some bad times at the inn, but her bleakest note may be a commentary on the impermanence of everything: "The inn burned down September 13, 1934," she said.

LA PLAZA INN— After E. G. Lewis, the developer of Atascadero, was forced into bankruptcy, management was turned to Fred Bartholomew in 1926. The Inn served as the community's social center for many years.

LOUNGE. ATASCADERO INN, A BARTHOLOMEW HOTEL, EXACTLY HALF WAY BETWEEN SAN FRANCISCO AND LOS ANGELES

MISSION STYLE LOUNGE of Atascadero Inn sometime after 1926.

ATASCADERO INN after fire destroyed it September 13, 1934.

FIRST LADY of Atascadero Colony, Mrs. E. G. Lewis.

BEFORE PRESENT-DAY FOUR-LANE HIGHWAY 101 was constructed, traffic passed through Main Street in Atascadero. This card was printed in the 1930's.

PRESENT-DAY ATASCADERO ADMINISTRATION BUILDING provides space for Atascadero Historical Society Museum, Police Station, and City Administration.

ATASCADERO BEACH and MORRO BAY

The Most Beautiful Beach on the Pacific Coast

Copyright International Film Co.

A HIGHLY RESTRICTED SEASIDE RESORT FOR NICE PEOPLE

Atascadero Beach Land & Improvement Company

Lewis Foundation Corporation

Sw. Luth. Church and Hall, Templeton, Cal.

SWEDISH LUTHERAN CHURCH— It began with the town of Templeton.

A PASTOR'S CHILD IN TEMPLETON

Astrid Berg was 2-1/2 years old when she arrived in Templeton with her younger brother, Phillip, and her parents, Reverend and Mrs. Petrus Berg. It was late afternoon, Nov. 18, 1909. Her father had been called as the new pastor to the Swedish Evangelical Lutheran Bethel Church.

"A large group of people from the church met us at the railroad station," she said. She quotes from a letter written by her father: "I thought I was dreaming. It was midwinter in Minnesota, but here the sun was shining, the grass was green, roses and other flowers were blooming. It was heavenly."

This was the beginning of Astrid's life in Templeton, and she disclosed many happy memories in a publication celebrating the first 100 years of our postcard church. The building had been constructed soon after the division of the southern portion of the El Paso de Robles Rancho and the development of the Templeton townsite in 1886.

On the evening of July 27, 1887, a group of 20 newly arrived Swedish settlers gathered at the home of Mr. and Mrs. August "Smed" Johnson for coffee and discussion about organizing a church. Chauncey Hatch Phillips, the manager of the West Coast Land Company, undoubtedly helped their cause by placing ads in several Swedish language church publications in the midwest urging settlement in Templeton. These ads brought more Swedish Lutherans.

In June, 1888, the acting trustees filed articles of incorporation with the San Luis Obispo county clerk, and in 1890, the congregation purchased a lot. Carl Carlson, the architect, planned a church with simple lines reminiscent of the churches of his native Sweden, and volunteer workers made the bricks for the building using clay from the Salinas River bottom. Lay pastor J. A. Levin had been a woodcarver in Sweden. He carved the beautiful redwood altar and pulpit still in use a century later.

The church was opened for its first

service in early 1891, drawing 170 people. That same year, the trustees purchased five acres for a cemetery.

In 1906, the Young People's Society, later known as the Bethel Church Luther League, gave the church a bell made in Troy, New York. This gift led to the construction of a belfry over the vestibule.

In 1909, the year that little Astrid and her family arrived in Templeton, the trustees announced that the church was at last free of all debt.

Astrid's mother was both organist and choir director. At first, she played a foot-pump organ. Later, a hand pump was used to fill the bellows. Mrs. Berg also decorated the altar with flowers from her garden every Sunday. She loved her garden so much, Astrid said, that when frost threatened her Chrysanthemums one winter, she used all of the sheets and towels in the parsonage to cover them.

The family had a horse named Mellie. "My father would hitch Mellie to a large buggy with front and back seats to go visiting members of the congregation" who lived on farms in the surrounding area. "I can remember going to sleep to the clip-clop of Mellie's hoofs.."

"When butchering time came we had a pioneer-type party when folks gathered to help skin, cut meat, make sausage, and `try out' the fat for lard." Without refrigeration, the women fried the chops and sausage patties and put them in crocks layered with lard. The meat kept that way all winter.

"Every summer the congregation traveled in a long wagon train along Santa Rita road for a camp-out at Morro Bay," Astrid remembered. "Everyone piled blankets, food and cooking utensils into horse-drawn buggies and wagons for the day-long trek. Most of us slept in makeshift tents set up in a Eucalyptus grove above the sand dunes."

There was one especially memorable day in 1918. When Astrid and her little brother heard the news, they ran to the church, climbed into the belfry and hung on both ropes, swinging and tugging to ring the bell so that the whole settlement would know that it was time to celebrate. The armistice had come. World War I was over.

TEMPLETON SCHOOL— It was finally torn down in 1923. While the new school was built, students attended classes in the Swedish Lutheran Fellowship Hall.

Templeton School, Templeton, Cal.

Veranda of Hotel, Paso Robles Hot Springs, Cal.

VERANDA, EL PASO DE ROBLES HOTEL— Guests relax in suits and hats in sturdy rockers.

PASO ROBLES OFFERED BUBBLING HOT SPRINGS AND SPREADING OAKS

Maybe Dan and James Blackburn already knew about the many hot springs on one portion of the 26,000-acre El Paso de Robles Rancho when they bought it in 1857. Certainly the priests and Indians at Mission San Miguel had made good use of them through the years. In any case, these bubbling hot sulphur waters became the nucleus of an impressive stage coach era resort and health center as well as the site for the City of Paso Robles and the classy El Paso de Robles Hotel shown in so many old picture postcards.

The Blackburn brothers came from Illinois. They were already experienced farmers, carpenters and mill hands when they bought the rancho from its Mexican grantee, Petronillo Rios.

They soon constructed a small hotel with a number of cabins, and dug a pool near the hot springs, enclosing it in a small building. The "curative" waters brought patients from near and far.

In 1864, a reporter for the San Francisco Bulletin described life at the hot springs as "badly crippled, walking on crutches and hobbling about with canes."

That same year Edward Vischer stopped at the hotel and sketched what he saw. His work shows two buildings, a single-story and a two-story. The larger one appears to have been the hotel.

Both Blackburn brothers remained single until finally, when fifty years old, Dan Blackburn married Cecilia Dunn in a double-wedding ceremony. The other couple was Drury James, who married Louisa, Cecelia's sister. James soon bought a large interest in the hotel.

James had made his money driving cattle from Southern California to the mining country in earlier years. Now, he owned 10,000 acres in the La Panza district.

Interestingly, when the younger Blackburn died, he left all of his holdings to his brother's wife, Cecilia. Since he had never married, even family members speculated about his unrequited love for his sister-in-law.

The Southern Pacific Railroad built line past the hot springs hotel in 1886, so Blackburn and James began to expand their private wooden village into a city. They hired a planner to layout a townsite around the hotel, and through a series of auctions, sold town lots.

As Blackburn grew older, Drury James became the dominate partner. When the City of Paso Robles incorporated in February, 1889, James served as first president of the new Board of Trustees. During that year, James also unveiled plans for the grandest hotel in San Luis Obispo County. One hundred years later Paso Robles would carry out a year-long centennial celebration.

In September, a stringer for the San Luis Obispo Tribune wrote, "The new hotel looms up grandly now that the kitchen and dining room walls are done and work has been pushed so that the main front is halfway up the window sides."

Then the troubles began, and construction stopped. The half-finished hotel surrounded by the new town became a haunting reminder of a partnership dispute and serious financial difficulties.

EL PASO DE ROBLES HOTEL— The new building opened October, 1891. With the coming of the railroad in 1889, guests came from long distances and remained for extended periods.

c1910— GUESTS socialized and rested in this large airy room overlooking the gardens. Suffering from a variety of aches and pains , they enjoyed relief by soaking in the mud and hot spring baths.

THE GARDENS included many places for rest and conversation. Here, a swinging seat hanging from a limb of the large trees provides a place for reading and socializing.

Faulty construction also showed. Some of the brick work was obviously out of line and poorly laid over the arches of the building. The architect called for the brick's removal and other reconstruction.

In June, 1891, word spread throughout the county that Dan and Cecilia Blackburn had sold their interest in the hotel. Drury James became controlling shareholder in a new corporation. Now others shared in its ownership.

The new hotel opened October 12, 1891. Townspeople promenaded along the sixteen-foot wide veranda running around three sides of the three-story hotel. They enjoyed meals in the large dining hall, viewed the circular towers extending over the north and south wings and toured the large airy solarium constructed over the center of the building.

The ground floor included parlors, a billiard room, a reading room, club meeting rooms, a saloon and a barber shop. People were drawn to the hotel by advertisements appearing in Sunset and other magazines.

The new El Paso de Robles Hotel endured until 1940 when fire destroyed it. In its place stands the modern Paso Robles Inn with motel and restaurant built around tree-shaded gardens and pool. In the back, a large building now used as a warehouse once served as the elegant dining room for the El Paso de Robles Hotel.

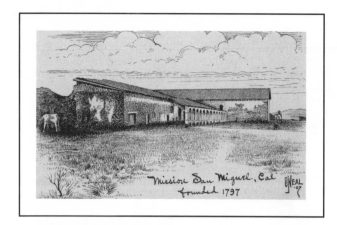

HIGHLIGHTS IN THE HISTORY OF
MISSION SAN MIGUEL

July 25, 1797- Founded as the sixteenth mission in the California chain by Padre Fermin Lasuen.

1806- A major fire destroyed the early mission structures. Workshops, granaries and all of the stored crops for feeding the large population of Indians were lost.

1816-18- The present church was built.

1820-21- Spanish artist Estevan Munras with several Indian assistants decorated the interior of the church.

1834- Secularization procedures began in this year. Even after government administrators informed the Indians that they were free, most of them declined to leave.

1845- Mission San Miguel buildings and surrounding lands were sold to Petronillo Rios and James Reid.

1848- James Reid and his family, occupying the south rooms of the mission that year, were all murdered by a band of men who had deserted a ship at Monterey. It is said that Reid had recently returned from the mining country with a cache of gold.

1859- Along with other missions, San Miguel was returned to the catholic church by the United States Land Commission.

1878- The mission buildings remained unused by the church for 36 years. Some space was rented to small stores.

JULY, 1897- Mission San Miguel celebrated its centennial. Large crowds attended this event.

1901- The mission buildings were renovated.

1928- The church was returned to the Franciscan Order for use as a parish church. Today, it is a compelling tourist attraction.

RIOS— Caledonia Adobe.

POST HARFORT CAL

NARROW GAUGE RAILS ACROSS THE RANCHOS

Hope Remained Dim for These California Landmen Until One Man Built a Horse-Drawn Railroad.

No wonder San Francisco newspapers sometimes referred to San Luis Obispo and Northern Santa Barbara Counties as the "gap", and no wonder the few settlers occupying these lands felt so doubtful about ever opening the territory to immigrants. It took a really seasoned and determined traveler to reach this area by either stagecoach or sea, even during the last quarter of the nineteenth century.

For one thing, settlers in the northern part of San Luis Obispo County were almost cut off from the southern part. The only connection was a precariously steep, curving and deeply rutted wagon trail winding through a pass known as La Cuesta in the Santa Lucias. Travel was nearly impossible in bad weather and dangerous at all times. San Marcos Pass created a similar problem for Santa Barbara County. Even the proximity of these counties to the sea was little comfort before 1870 because they lacked wharves for ready transfer of goods and passengers to and from ships plying the coast.

The first editor of the San Luis Obispo Tribune, Walter Murray, described the difficulty of his arrival in the San Luis Obispo mission settlement by sea in 1853 aboard the Steamer Sea Bird in this way: "The purser handed (me) the great U.S. mail, which we had no difficulty concealing in our pocket." Then Murray went over the side of the steamer into a waiting lighter, and crew members rowed him ashore.

"Luckily, the sea was not very rough, and we therefore did not get wet; but on landing at the extremity of a long stretch of...beach, (I found) not a soul... nor any sign of habitation, save a house in the distance." He was given shelter at the house, and the next day he made his way on foot for about 10 miles to the mission and scattered adobe dwellings of the San Luis Obispo settlement.

Some settlers, including Murray, complained in letters to families about the area, but cheap land and the ties property can create kept a few enterprising anglos struggling along with a much larger group of Californios and families, all hoping for much more.

Whatever fervor they shared with other Californians about the completion of the transcontinental railroad in 1869 was quickly dashed. The Southern Pacific Railroad began laying connecting track out of the San Francisco bay area toward Los Angeles through the inland valley rather than along the coast.

This situation may explain why the people in this coastal territory came to see John Harford in somewhat heroic proportions. He took the inital steps that would open the world for them. In early August, 1874, the Santa Barbara News Press printed a long biographical article about him. On August 15, the San Luis Obispo Tribune reprinted it.

In part, it read: "We call him a hero, and we wish to introduce him to.. (our)..readers. He is "a plain, honest man, most modest and simple-hearted, of moderate means and limited educational advantages." But Harford's achievements defy such a description. His inventiveness and dogged efforts began a progressive movement that altered economic conditions in these backward counties for years to come.

At the time, Harford was manager of Swartz-Harford Company, a small retail lumber business. In order to take delivery of his company's products from Santa Cruz and other coastal lumber manufacturing ports, small freighters anchored as close to the

PADDLE WHEEL Steamer Senator— Courtesy National Maritime Museum, San Francisco.

beach as they dared, and at high tide they tossed the lumber that he ordered overboard. Incoming tides washed the boards to the beach, and with the help of a few Chinese laborers, Harford stacked it, loaded it on wagons and took it to a drying yard. It worked, but at best, some lumber went astray and some boards must have wound up warped and buckled.

In December, 1868, Harford joined forces with the Goldtree Brothers and A. Blockman and Company. His new partners operated small general stores in San Luis Obispo and came to play key roles in a variety of area business ventures. With Harford in charge of work crews, they built an 1800-foot wharf from the sandy beach of San Miguelito Rancho far enough into San Luis Obispo bay to allow most steamships of the time to actually tie-up. Then they constructed a warehouse above the beach where farmers could store their grain and other produce while

waiting for ships to take it to big city markets. They called their new development the People's Wharf.

Although Harford joined his partners in an area-wide celebration after completion of the wharf in early September, 1869, he had serious regrets about the spot where it had been constructed. Against his judgment, his partners had insisted upon this beach location because of its easy access and because it was the least expensive construction site. Blockman soon bought Harford's interest in the wharf and continued expanding it into still deeper water. The wharf actually accommodated some of the largest ships in the trade. Three lines began to call regularly at this wharf. The Pacific Mail Steamship Company had three vessels making stops as they sailed between San Francisco and San Diego: the Mohongo, the Orizaba and the Gypsy. Then, in November, 1873, Goodall, Nelson and Perkins announced that their steamers,

Ventura and Constantine, would stop for freight and passengers every Sunday, one going south and the other north. Their Kalorama would "touch in fortnightly."

In addition, another old steamer began making spasmodic stops. It was owned by John Wright, the celebrated opposition pirate and owner of the William Tabor. Most locals held him in contempt. They knew he hoped to either sell out to or blackmail the regular lines, and he gained his patronage only from others like himself.

"Our port and county are both established institutions..let us favor substantial lines...rather than the ephemeral and desultory efforts of a mere blackmailer," the Tribune advised.

All this time, Harford visualized a wharf about a mile farther north, located closer to the lee side of Point San Luis, well protected from northwest trade winds and heavy breakers. Of course, his partners had ignored his pleas for good reasons of their own. What he wanted to do would cost too much money.

"...this (location) was at least a mile from any (level) accessible point on the bay, the whole distance being walled in by a rough, serrated rocky bluff," the Press told its readers.

Most people knew Harford lacked financial means for such an undertaking:. "...he had only a small capital and the people had little faith or interest in the project." Still, if John Harford was a simple man, he didn't know it. Rather quietly, it seems, he gained access and right-of-way to the land he would need and prepared to go to work.

But Harford could not do this job alone. Fortunately, another equally quiet but competent man appeared on the scene. The Santa Barbara Press didn't mention the new man nor fully know the implications of what they wrote when they said, "John went..to work with a handful of Chinamen, and (they) cut away the rocky projections, spanned the chasms with trestle work and laid down ties of half-length redwood fence posts..spiked on small iron T-nails." The fact is that Harford had a Chinese labor boss he called Ah Luis and a Chinese crew with experience at railroad building. Harford had hired them to build a narrow gauge railway along the bluff to the wharf site. He planned to lay about a mile of track.

According to family tradition, this leader among the Chinese took the name of Ah Louis. From discussions between the author and the late Young Louis, the eldest son, along with physical facts in evidence, we know that Ah Louis became one of the early businessmen in this remote area and the father of a large and respected family. Upon him would fall the task of recruiting and contracting Chinese labor for a variety of major local projects.

Under Harford's direction, Ah Louis' men laid track along the precipice of the bay from the site of the planned wharf to level land near the People's Wharf where farmers could conveniently load and unload their wagons. To everyone's amazement, Harford used his workers to also construct the first of his wooden flatbed rail cars to which they attached factory-made cast-iron axles and wheels. Then, they built the Harford wharf about 400 feet out into the bay to reach deep water. All things considered, his work proved a masterful job. A few years later, the People's Wharf was partially destroyed by a storm, but Harford's Wharf remained steadfast, proving his fears about the location of the first wharf well-founded.

"In this unostentious and straight-forward manner," the Press told its readers back in 1874, "cheered on by a few worthy

Light House at Port San Luis, Cal.

friends..Mr. Harford soon had his railroad and wharf in operation. "It (is) the first narrow-gauge railroad in Southern California." Of course, Harford didn't have an engine to pull his cars, but that didn't stop him. He used horses.

A reporter from the Tribune took a ride with Harford over his line, describing the experience. A team of horses started from the location of the company's warehouse in what is now the town of Avila. They pulled a flat car with seats up to the summit of the hill in the direction of Harford's wharf.   Here, Harford unhitched the team, and gravity took care of the downhill part of the trip. The cars coasted through a tunnel and down a steep grade to the water's edge and then around a curve onto the wharf. During the trip, Harford stood at the brake controls slowing the speed as necessary down the incline.

With a "force of five men, three horses and two little trains of cars" he could "move 50,000 feet of lumber in one 10-hour day." By standards of the past in this vicinity, Harford had revolutionized lumber and freight handling.

And Ah Louis had proven the value of Chinese laborers in the region, and perhaps more important at the time, the economy of using them. There was still plenty of track to be laid in the area, but Ah Louis also turned to other enterprises. In addition to his labor contracting business, he operated a brick-making yard which inspired local builders to construct many downtown buildings of brick rather than wood as in the past. It would not be until September 4, 1885, that the Tribune would announce that the "Ah Lui" brick building at the corner of Chorro and Palm streets was nearing completion and that he would soon be able "to accommodate his many past customers." San Luis Obispo's

Chinatown developed along this block. Today, the Ah Louis building continues in use as an oriental gift shop under the management of grandson Howard Louis, and it is identified as a California state historical landmark.

John Harford's initiative began a series of progressive efforts. With two wharves now available on the San Miguelito Rancho, Juan Avila and his brothers announced plans for a new town at the terminal point of Harford's horse-drawn railroad and the beach where the People's Wharf was located. A plot plan signed by their mother, Inocenta, and prepared by R. R. Harris, the county surveyor, provided for a town plan showing five broad streets. Prospective buyers were invited to study the town site map at the county surveyors office or at the People's Landing. These coastal lots could be purchased at 20 percent down and 10 percent interest, the balance payable in one year. A new coastal community was in the making.

The Avila brothers and their mother had inherited the San Miguelito Rancho from the early head of the household, Don Miguel Avila after his death February 24, 1874). Don Miguel had received the rancho as a grant from Mexican Governor Juan Bautista Alvarado in two parcels dated April 8, 1839 and May 10, 1842. The rancho covered 22,136 acres.) The new townsite was less than 200 acres along the beachfront.

Other good things happened during those first years after construction of the wharves. For one thing, the San Luis Obispo County Courthouse had been located in a crumbling two-story adobe house built 20 years earlier by William Goodwin Dana, grantee of the 37,000-acre Nipomo Rancho. But in 1873, construction of a substantial

STEAMSHIP SANTA ROSA, Pacific Coast Steamship Company- One of many vessels carrying both passengers and freight between ports along the California coast.

new three-story courthouse promised to change the outlook of the whole community. And after so many years, both the Episcopalians and the Methodists began construction of churches, the first protestant churches in the town. The Episcopalians dedicated their new church building October 5, 1873.

Then during 10 days of September in that year, Bishop Thaddeus Amat, acting for the Catholic Church, sold more than a block of lots in the former mission gardens that opened new level lands for the future city. A number of families planned two-story houses in this new garden area. Among them,

1905-
Summer Tub
Gowns for
Comfortable
Travel.

Chauncey Hatch Phillips. Phillips was a newcomer with exceptional charisma and extraordinary ideas about the future of the county.

He would gradually show the whole county how to capitalize on its assets. He and his wife, Jane, came from Fond de Lac, Wisconsin. After arriving in California in 1862, he worked for the U.S. Internal Revenue in Napa, San Jose and San Francisco. Tall, lean and commanding in appearance, he proved unusually able in financial affairs, and he came to positions of leadership easily and quickly.

Soon after his arrival, he met Horatio Moore Warden. Warden and his brother, Lew, each owned large ranches on the old Canada de Los Osos Rancho, land originally purchased from it Mexican grantee by the late Shipmaster John Wilson.

Warden and Phillips joined forces to establish the county's first bank. They called it the San Luis Obispo Bank. Phillips first served as its manager while Warden, the principal investor, was its president. It didn't take them long to decide to expand their operations through incorporation and additional capitalization of $200,000. Major stockholders included D. W. James, one of the owners of the Paso Robles Hot Springs on the El Paso de Robles Rancho; E. W. and George Steele, owners of large land holdings on four different Mexican land grants..the Arroyo Grande, the Bolsa de Chamisal, the Corral de Piedra and the El Pismo, all located in Southern San Luis Obispo County; J. P. Andrews, a hog rancher and local capitalist who had given the land for the county courthouse; William Beebee of the firm of Schwartz, Harford and Company; and none other than John Harford, the wharf and horse-drawn railway builder. After this quick expansion, chief executive Warden retired and Phillips became the bank's president. It was only the beginning for Phillips.

Harford's inspired vision along with Ah Louis' leadership in recruiting Chinese labor from San Francisco had made real what other local businessmen had not dreamed possible without large capital. But now, some of them joined forces with Harford, hoping to fulfill a long held mutual dream..a railroad with a real engine and track all of the way from the port into San Luis Obispo, less than 10 miles away.

For a brief time under the leadership of David Norcross, a group of local businessmen began holding regular meetings, discussing the prospect of building a narrow gauge railroad into town. We do not know whether these men were serious about their discussions or whether they had heard rumors about outside interests making similar plans. Perhaps they simply wanted a piece of the action.

Norcross was elected president of the group, and he began securing right-of-way contracts across land between the port and town. The group even hired some workers and staked out a route, doing a little grading.

Maybe they anticipated what happened

1905—Millinery for the spring traveler.

next. Word reached San Luis Obispo through an item published in the San Francisco Evening Bulletin that their area's state senator, William J. Graves, had introduced a bill authorizing the construction of "a railroad from San Luis Obispo Bay to Santa Maria in Santa Barbara County." An entirely different group of men sponsored this bill. Except for holding some legal right-of-way contracts, Norcross and his people were soon out of business.

The new incorporators included Charles Goodall and C. Nelson of Goodall, Nelson and Perkins Steamship Company. It appeared that the much discussed railroad might have some money behind it. Local men of the company included Juan Avila of the San Miguelito Rancho whose land would have to be crossed to reach San Luis Obispo; John Price, owner of a portion of the El Pizmo Rancho; Nathan Goldtree, a partner with his brothers in Goldtree Brothers, a general store in San Luis Obispo; and some lesser known men. They planned to call their line the San Luis Obispo and Santa Maria Railroad.

We "unreservedly applaud the enterprise and commend the sterling worth and financial ability of the gentlemen whose names appear as incorporators," the Tribune said. "They will require no county subsidy or contributions from private citizens..." But Editor Rembaugh did not know what was coming when he so confidently prognosticated the future.

It took some time for area settlers to know the backgrounds of the steamship principals investing in this project. All three had started at the bottom of the financial and social world, according to the San Francisco Chronicle of January 17, 1875, working themselves into their successful positions. Goodall had arrived in San Francisco in 1850. During the early part of his career, he served

PORT HARFORD about 1910— Shows engine and boxcar with steamer docked at the end.

as agent for the Sausalito Water and Steam Tug Company, the Bensley Water Company and the Spring Valley Water Company. Each of these organizations grew out of or were merged with the others. In 1864 and 1866, he was elected harbor master for San Francisco and during 1870-71, he served in the state assembly. He and Christopher Nelson formed a ship towing company in 1860, also providing Spring Valley water to ships coming and going in port. Slowly, they accumulated small vessels and began shipping along the coast.

Nelson had arrived in California as master of the trading brig, William Penn Nelson. Later, he served as master of the sternwheeler Oroville. "He is a shrewd, kind and sensible man," the Chronicle wrote at the beginning of 1875. He carried a deep scar on his head resulting from a wound he received during a mutiny on board a vessel while he served as its mate during his early years at sea.

The third partner in the steamship company was George C. Perkins. Perkins was the fulltime politician in the partnership. He began his career in California in 1856 by driving a grocery wagon in Oroville, eventually owning Perkins and Company, a wholesale grocery and liquor firm. In 1872, Butte County elected him as its representative in the California State Senate. Perkins was described as an unusually affable and handsome man. He became rich in the wholesale grocery and liquor business. He was elected State Senator at about the same time he invested in the steamship company. His activities in state politics would bring him to the governor's chair in 1880. Still later, he would fill the unexpired term of Leland Stanford as United States Senator.

It is worth noting that while this little railroad gained legal status in the legislature, the lieutenant governor of California was Romualdo Pacheco, a resident and landowner in San Luis Obispo County. Any railway built between San Luis Obispo and Santa Maria would likely cross the Suey Rancho, land granted to Pacheco's mother by Governor Alvarado in 1837. During the 1873 session of the legislature, Pacheco, while presiding over the state senate, sought and gained Senator Grave's vote to elect Governor Newton Booth as United States Senator. Now, both Governor Booth and Lieutenant Governor Pacheco, though Dolly Varden Republicans, owed Democrat Graves whatever assistance he needed for getting a railroad built in the area he represented.

Reconstruction of the narrow gauge line would have to begin again at Harford's wharf, this time with rails that would accommodate the weight of an engine. Seeking assurance that work was underway, Tribune Editor Rembaugh and R. R. Harris, the county surveyor, took a buckboard down to Avila landing in mid-September, 1874.

"There we found a thousand feet of trestle work.." constructed "under a Mr. Osgood, a master workman," Rembaugh reported. The company planned construction all of the way to San Luis Obispo, the Tribune editor assured his readers.

PARTY GIRLS—Off to a Dance party in Nipomo.

During this time, the newspaper was also filled with news items about all of the other good things happening in the area, and once again John Harford was praised for demonstrating that a railroad was possible and financially worthwhile. As part of the opening of the territory, the Western Union Telegraph Company reached town, and a man named Joe Frederi had leased the old wooden French Hotel at the corner of Monterey and Chorro Streets across from the mission, refurbished it and now announced the opening of its restaurant and rooms.

On October 13, 1874, James Blackburn, half-owner of the El Paso de Robles Rancho, announced the grand opening of his new 30-room Cosmopolitan Hotel in the very center of downtown San Luis Obispo.

"There were processions of people coming in from the surrounding country with smiling faces and flounced dresses.." the Tribune reported. They toured the sleeping rooms, the parlors, the reading room and the saloon. Some of the men really enjoyed the two fine billiard tables.

The place was brilliantly "illuminated" with gaslights, and Pico's string band provided music in the dining area for dancing quadrilles, waltzes, polkas and all the other popular dances of the day.

"The heel and toe was all the go, and that is so, as all should know, that ever went to a dance with a beau," the reporter frivolously reported. Supper was served at midnight with desserts including "pyramidal cakes covered with sugar frost..and then tart and mince pies." There had not been quite such an area celebration in years.

The Catholic Church contracted for an "asphaltum paved promenade in front of Mission San Luis Obispo, introducing for the first time in the area, the extraordinary merit of paved walkways and streets in place of the

1910—TOWN OF AVILA with Pacific Coast Railroad trestle in foreground and wharf in distance.

dusty rutted ones of the past. Within months, the city begain grading and graveling the two main streets, Monterey and Higuera, along with their cross streets. Then, on each side of these streets, they laid asphaltum sidewalks. In this town of less than 2,000 population, paved walkways were viewed as remarkable. Some people saw pavement for the first time in their lives. Best of all, the new product came from asphaltum rock quarried in the Edna Valley only a few miles from home.

As 1874 ended, John Harford told a reporter that two twelve-ton engines had been ordered, and on behalf of Goodall, Nelson and Perkins Steamship Company, he said he soon planned to hire 300 men to begin construction toward San Luis Obispo. It would not be long, the newspaper said, before townspeople would hear the sound of "the whistle of the Iron Horse."

It was on March 26, 1875 that ground was officially broken for the San Luis Obispo and Santa Maria Railroad in the new town of Avila. L.H. Shoutt, chief engineer, announced that the Steamer San Luis had arrived in port carrying a crew of laborers from San Francisco. It was another time of jubilation in the territory.

About two months passed after Shoutt's announcement, and as people traveled along the wagon road between town and the landing during this time, they brought back some very disheartening news. Nothing was happening along the right-of-way. As a matter of fact, someone associated with the steamship company intimated that the road would not be built into town unless the railroad was paid a subsidy.

"The people of this place have suffered so much (for) so long and so patiently from the shortcomings of the steamship companies," Editor Rembaugh told his readers, "that forbearance ceases to be a virtue."

The story discussed the unreliability of the steamship arrivals and departures and the generally shabby treatment people experienced at the management's hands. Then, the story assumed a threatening tone. It mentioned that the Southern Pacific Railroad had finished laying track as far south as Soledad in 1873, so "if the people are to pay subsidies..they will pay..to have the coast (railroad) extended from Soledad..for they would then have a certainty before them."

Apparently, Goodall, Nelson and Perkins did not pursue community subsidies very far. Instead, the corporation sought capitalization through local stock sales. John Harford had had his day as hero in the area. Now, Chauncey Hatch Phillips took a turn.

As president of the bank, he obtained the books of the railway company and opened them to potential investors. He immediately began promoting and selling stock to all comers. The steamship company had already subscribed to $30,000 worth of the railroad's stock. Blockman and Company and Goldtree Brothers, with their investment in the People's Wharf, each invested $5,000. The railroad company said they needed $50,000 to buy all of John Harford's interest, build rail line into San Luis Obispo and purchase rolling stock. "Will our rich men take hold of the matter and make the road a success or must we go on into the future..through dust, mud and floods..to reach the landing (using wagons)?" Editor Rembaugh asked?

Phillips did not wait for prospective investors to come to him. Active in every business and social organization, he enthusi-

THIS TRESTLE CROSSED San Luis Obispo Creek. It existed until 1981 when it fell during a storm.

astically discussed the merits of the narrow gauge railway stock with everyone he met. He enlisted the help of C. H. Johnson, owner of land in the town's business district as well as the surrounding area, and Johnson also sold stock.

During this time there was a fortuitous announcement that may have helped spur some stock sales. The Tribune noted that the Southern Pacific Railroad would soon build track out of Soledad toward San Miguel in northern San Luis Obispo County. Editor Rembaugh suggested that the San Luis and Santa Maria Valley Railway could then build a line through the Cuesta Pass to meet the Southern Pacific. Such a statement was speculation of the wildest kind, but in the heat of things, he apparently got by with it.

"With the building of railroads will come an influx of settlers..only too glad to buy all the surplus land adapted to agriculture and thus in a comparative short time quadruple our population and wealth," he told his readers.

By now, a man named John Farrell served as superintendent of the railway. To overcome complaints people had sent to State Senator William Graves, he wrote a letter to the legislator dated July 30, 1875 discussing the company's intentions. "We intend to complete the road (rail line) from Avila to Castros within the next sixty days, always with the intention of continuing the road to San Luis Obispo, as soon as we have funds available for that purpose," he told the senator.

Castro's Place (later called Harford and then Miles Station) was a spot on a ranch about 3-1/2 miles inland from Avila. A warehouse and loading platform at this location would eliminate the need of farmers hauling produce all of the way to either San Luis Obispo or Avila.

"We have already laid out..money for grading, iron, etc. We have also ordered an eighteen-ton locomotive from Philadelphia, and the Kimball Manufacturing Company (is) now making..ten freight cars and a passenger car.." Farrell's letter to Senator Graves continued. "To complete the road from Castro's to San Luis together with depot buildings will require about $50,000. If we can get that amount subscribed, we would continue the road to town without delay..If we have to rely on our own resources, we will be unable to do so this season."

In mid-September, Rembaugh accepted an invitation from railroad Superintendent Farrell and Christopher Nelson of

THE PEOPLE'S WHARF COMPANY OF SAN LUIS OBISPO,

WOULD call the attention of citizens of San Luis Obispo to the superior facilities offered by them to shippers of Produce and Merchandize to and from the Port of San Luis Obispo, by their

LARGE AND COMMODIOUS WAREHOUSES AND WHARF.

Vessels of all kinds can lay at the wharf, and discharge and load cargo. Two large Warehouses have been erected for the receipt and storage of Produce and Merchandize. A gentlemanly and accommodating Wharfinger will be constantly in attendance, to take charge of and account for freight. Produce will be shipped by any conveyance the shipper may desire.

All outward freight will be stored thirty days free of charge; inward freight for fifteen days.

The following rates of wharfage have been fixed as legal charges by the Board of Supervisors of the county at this wharf:

Grain and Vegetables,	per	ton,	$0 60
Lumber,	"	M.	1 00
Shakes,	"	"	25
Shingles,	"	"	12½
Posts,	"	bun.	1 00
Wool,	"	ton,	1 00
Laths,	"	M.,	15
Hides,	"	each,	1
Cheeses,	"	"	2
Hogs, Sheep and Calves,	"	"	5
Horses,	"	"	1 00
Horned Cattle,	"	"	25
For each one or two horse vehicle,			1 00
For each four or six " "			2 00

On all inward freight not specified in the above schedule, ONE DOLLAR per ton. Outward freight, SEVENTY-FIVE CENTS per ton.

A share of the public patronage is respectfully solicited. 35-tf.

Goodall, Nelson and Perkins to inspect the progress of the railway. "At the new town of Harford (Castro's Place), five miles below San Luis," Rembaugh saw the new graded six-foot wide railway bed. He was impressed with the many culverts that flowed water under the roadbed. Out of the developing town of Avila, he saw 6"x8" railway ties supporting "T-rail 42 pounds to the yard, much heavier than most rail used with narrow-gauge lines."

Rembaugh was told that the company would soon build a bridge 300 feet in length across the mouth of San Luis Obispo Creek at Avila. At the company's office in Avila, he witnessed and inspected topographical maps detailing railway construction plans into San Luis Obispo and then to Arroyo Grande, Nipomo, Santa Maria, Los Alamos and finally into a non-existing town in the Santa Ynez Valley. Ultimately, he was told, the company expected to serve Lompoc and Santa Barbara. This line, Rembaugh suggested, could even connect with the Southern Pacific's valley line at Bakersfield someday. This eye witness report of something on paper pro-vided some very heady visualizing at a time when every local person's dreams fed off those of others.

During the latter half of 1875, local leaders gradually realized that if their area became all they wanted, they must have a breakwater to further protect their harbor and the ship's tying up at the wharves. U.S. Congressman P. D. Wigginton followed up their pleas by introducing legislation for a federal appropriation of $150,000 for a break-water and lighthouse. He advised them of the need to send someone back to Washington D. C. to help lobby for their needs. At the time, one of their own citizens, Governor Romualdo Pacheco neared the end of his term. He readily accepted an invitation to go to Wash-ington on behalf of the county to talk to congressmen about harbor improvements. Chauncey Hatch Phillips along with Dr. H. H. Hays and L. Landeker agreed to act as a liason committee between Governor Pacheco in Washington and local citizens in providing whatever support was needed. No end of effort was required but local leaders appeared to thrive on it.

AVILA LIGHT-HOUSE still remains above Port San Luis. Lighthouse keeper lived in the Victorian structure. This building will be preserved by the Port San Luis Authority.

SEPTEMBER, 1889—Steamship Los Angeles, a passenger and freight vessel operated by the Pacific Coast Steamship Company. This steamer made regular stops at Port San Luis and Santa Barbara.

On Tuesday evening, December 28, a citizen's meeting was called at Little and Cappe's Hall and Saloon. State Senator Graves and Governor Pacheco both spoke. George Perkins, state senator from Butte County and a principal in the Pacific Coast Steamship Company was also present to express his favor concerning the potential appropriation.

Senator Graves told the group that he recalled Captain John Wilson, Pacheco's stepfather, telling of a Pacific storm twenty years earlier that forced him to bring his brig into San Luis Obispo Bay. Wilson had called the bay the safest refuge for ships between San Francisco and San Diego.

Governor Pacheco came to the rostrum amid warm and appreciative applause. He recalled the gales of the Pacific Coast when he sailed in his stepfather's vessels, and he told about losing dear friends while battling the waves off the coast of San Luis Obispo Bay. He considered construction of a breakwater completely feasible, he told the crowd.

George Perkins, a future governor of California and United States senator, also gave an inspiring speech, helping his audience visualize their dreams of a great and prosperous area with a first-class port and a railroad reaching all of the way to the San Joaquin Valley. But for all of the excitement about the possibility of a breakwater, residents faced disappointment. Congress failed to pass a bill providing funds for it, and absolutely nothing happened for many years.

By February 19, 1876 people's thoughts turned to more immediate business. Chauncey Hatch Phillips and C. H. Johnson announced that they had successfully obtained subscriptions to stock for the San Luis Obispo and Santa Maria Railroad amounting to $25,000. This amount was half what the company had originally requested, but somehow officials decided they could lay track to San Luis Obispo with the lesser amount.

Rumors and hopes for continuation of Southern Pacific line from Soledad and along the coast continued, but a decade must pass before this would happen. Nonetheless, there were causes for celebration in the year 1876. At a session of the California Senate on February 17, Senator Graves introduced an act for the incorporation of the City of San Luis Obispo, and in April, the new city held its first election.

Then, at long last in the issue of Saturday, August 5, 1876, Tribune Editor Rembaugh announced the news all had been waiting to hear. For three years now, Rembaugh had taken countless trips to Avila, reporting whatever he saw or did not see along the route between town and the landing. In his personalized reporting style, he complimented those who contributed in anyway to advancing the railway and scolded those who fell short of their duty. He assumed the role of arbiter of every dispute, the cheerleader in every forward movement and the compromiser when all other alternatives failed. In his role as editor and publisher of the small weekly newspaper, he, too, contributed immensely to the determined efforts of the local people for construction of the little railway.

So, he must have felt great satisfaction that week as he composed the story, line after line, directly into his composition stick telling the county that the first leg of the great task was all but completed. "By Monday evening," he wrote, "the last rail will have been laid and the cars will be running in town. ...we congratulate our people...we likewise congratulate the stockholders. From this time forward no more blockades by flood, no more sticking in the mud, no more sweltering in the dust, no more long hours ride in reaching the seashore." He encouraged the rail-

1910—PORT SAN LUIS with boxcars of Pacific Coast Railroad.

STEAMSHIP EUREKA—This Pacific Coast Steamship made regular stops at Port San Luis and Santa Barbara at the beginning of this century.

road managers to establish a passenger fare of not more than $1.00 roundtrip to encourage "excursions" to the beach.

The year was 1876. The great Philadelphia Centennial celebration of the Declaration of Independence was underway. Rembaugh sent copies of his newspaper to an agent that year for distribution in the Pacific Coast Hall. He wanted the world to know that San Luis Obispo County was a very progressive place. Its county seat was now an incorporated city, and a railroad operated between it and a Pacific port.

Almost incidentally, Mission San Luis Obispo, named for Saint Louis, the bishop of Toulouse, planned a celebration for its patron saint. Rembaugh hoped the railroad company would combine the grand opening of its line with this mission event by offering a community excursion to Avila. In this same month of August only seven years earlier, the first issue of the Tribune had been published.

Its publisher wanted a celebration that merged all the good things occurring in the lives of the people of the county. He wanted to call it San Luis Day.

But the celebration did not occur as Rembaugh suggested. Instead, new railroad Superintendent Joseph W. Nesbitt asked a committee of local company stockholders to plan a celebration. This committee recommended an excursion for Wednesday, August 23, limiting the number of participants to 300, including stockholders and their invited guests. In addition to the train ride, they scheduled a basket picnic in a grove enroute, band music and time to enjoy the beach in Avila. It was a family affair with many children. For most, it was their first train ride.

Year after year, Rembaugh and other local leaders continued urging construction of a rail line between the coast and Bakersfield. They wanted to somehow make a connection between the coast and Southern

Pacific's line through the San Joaquin Valley. But years of speculation about its possibilities could not overcome the reality of practical business. Railroad investors did not see any profit in undertaking the venture.

Still, the little narrow gauge railroad coming and going in San Luis Obispo and meeting the steamships at Port Harford provided a fresh breath of life in this otherwise isolated coastal area. When the Steamship Orizaba was pulled from service and brought back fully refurbished, people could read with relish about the party held aboard it in San Francisco Bay.

Later, when this same vessel was detained while taking on freight at Port Harford during one of its coastal trips, its through passengers from Southern California ports were "treated to an excursion on the narrow gauge to San Luis Obispo."

Patrick Murphy, former state senator and owner of the Santa Margarita Rancho, happened to be in town when the passengers arrived at the depot. He immediately invited a group to join him in a tour of the mission and the town. Another group visited the court-house, and Sheriff Oaks showed them through the county jail. These very beautifully dressed people from other places, about 25 or 30 of them, must have given San Luis Obispans something to talk about for days.

Five years passed before the Pacific Coast Railway decided to continue line beyond San Luis Obispo. In May, 1881, Charles Goodall gave orders to begin construction of track south to Central City (Santa Maria). The contractors announced that they had wanted to complete the job "exclusively with white labor but owing to the unreliability of some of the white men, they have been compelled to engage a small gang of Chinamen." Ah Louis probably had even more laborers available if there was a place for them.

"They are kept to themselves and do not come in contact with the whites," the superintendent told the newspaper. The workers were divided into seven gangs, each with its own boss. Some 150 men and 60 teams were employed.

In anticipation of the railroad reaching the Arroyo Grande settlement, farmers in the surrounding country, including those on

1910 - AVILA- Pacific Coast narrow-gauge track on the outskirts of town. The bed is still evident alongside the main road.

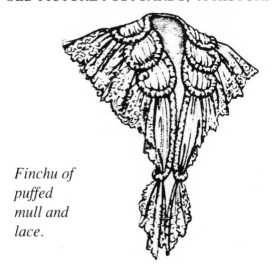

Finchu of puffed mull and lace.

LOOKING YOUR BEST aboard the steamer.

the great Nipomo Rancho, were already threshing. If the railroad did not finish its work on time, the farmers expected to send their grain by ship from the wharf nearing completion at Pismo.

What was referred to as the Arroyo Grande township had some of the most fertile soil in this whole central coast area. Even during early mission times, the priests and Indians of San Luis Obispo had maintained gardens in the vicinity. The population of the settlement in 1881 was about 200 people. The town already had a small hotel and stable, a general store and a school. The arrival of the railroad in the fall of 1881 soon led others to try their skills at various enterprises. The next year, the main street began to look like a real town with a new drug store, a another general store and a mill.

During this time, the San Francisco Examiner announced that the "princely Nipomo rancho had recently been purchased by George Hearst..." The story proved untrue, but some negotiations with the heirs of William Goodwin Dana, the original grantee, had apparently taken place. Hearst already owned large tracts of coastal land in the northern part of the county including San Simeon, Santa Rosa, and Piedra Blanca ran-

chos, all originally Mexican grants. These ranchos would one day be the site of the Hearst-San Simeon Historical Monument (Hearst's Castle on Highway 1).

The Examiner also noted that 20 flat cars and ten box cars would soon be shipped to Port Harford for service with the San Luis Obispo and Santa Maria Railroad.

Track was completed and freight trains began hauling to and from Arroyo Grande beginning October 12, 1881. Meantime, the railroad invited proposals for grading from Arroyo Grande to the Santa Maria River.

While this work proceeded, Charles Goodall traveled to Philadelphia where Cramp & Sons, a shipbuilding firm, was outfitting the Queen of the Pacific for addition to the fleet of Goodall, Nelson and Perkins. She was 336 feet long with a capacity for 2000 tons of cargo. She had 62 comfortable staterooms plus accommodations for 75 steerage passengers, a large dining room and a social hall.

But something strange was occurring. While local railroad work proceeded, no one heard anything from the principal owners of the steamship company. It was not until the end of the year that they dropped a bombshell that reverberated along the whole California coast. The San Francisco Call of November 30 and the San Luis Obispo Tribune of December 3, 1881 announced that Goodall, Nelson and Perkins had sold their interest to Henry Villard, president of the Oregon Navigation Company. They had taken this action without any word to other stockholders, creating some furor in company circles. They

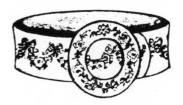

White silk buckle and belt. Embroidered with flowers.

sold stock originally worth $20 per share for $87.50 per share. With completion of this transaction, they continued as agents and managers for the steamship company and the railway. With fresh capital, the company undertook many improvements.

Almost coincidentally with construction of rails over the Nipomo Rancho, originally 37,000 acres, it was subdivided among the heirs of Captain William Dana and Maria Josepha Carrillo de Dana. Dana, a sea captain from Boston, had received this land as a grant from Mexican Governor Juan Bautista Alvarado April 6, 1837. When Dana died in 1858, the estate came fully under the ownership of his wife and was managed by her children. Of her 21 children, only 13 lived to adulthood. Now, in 1882, the children each received a tract of 1200 acres. They reserved another 12,000 acres as common property to be subdivided and sold in 400-500 acre parcels. One portion of the rancho known as Los Berros had been sold at an earlier time. At the heart of the rancho, they subdivided 160 acres into lots for the new town of Nipomo, naming all of the streets for members of the family and settlers of the area. Their site map for the town was submitted to the County of San Luis Obispo August 15, 1882.

"When the Pacific Coast Railroad came to Nipomo," the late Alonzo Dana, a grandson of William Goodwin and Maria Josepha Dana, wrote in a letter to the author, "the Danas gave them the right away across their land free except their mother could ride on the train free, but the only time she was on the train was when her body was taken to San Luis Obispo for burial in the Catholic Cemetery there."

After arrival of the railroad, a building was constructed in Nipomo known as the American House, Alonzo Dana said. There were five or six stores on the lower floor and the upstairs was a hotel. Fire destroyed this wooden structure in 1888. It was eventually replaced by other business buildings. The Nipomo News, a newspaper, was started by John Krider, an inlaw of the Danas, but it did not last long.

Even while the railway bridge was constructed across the Santa Maria River and track laid into the settlement of Santa Maria, a San Francisco dispatch dated April 17, 1882, reached the Santa Barbara News-Press saying that articles of incorporation had been filed for the operation of a railroad from the southern terminous of the San Luis Obispo and Santa Maria Railroad to the City of Santa Barbara with a capital stock of $2 million. The directors were none other than Charles and Edwin Goodall with William Norris and John Howard. These names were familiar to people of the area because all had a connection with the steamship company and the San Luis Obispo and Santa Maria Railroad. The San Luis Obispo Tribune reprinted the news story April 29, 1882.

But for some people, there were more exciting things happening. For example, one Saturday morning in April, the little railway

loaded nine cars full of picnickers, mostly school children, headed for Nipomo. Since they did not have that many passenger cars, they rigged up benches on some of their freight cars. The engineer may have blown the whistle a few extra times for the benefit of his passengers during that trip and its not hard to imagine the happy chatter and laughing that must have filled the cars as the train chugged through the Edna Valley and Corbett Canyon for its first stop at Arroyo Grande. Here, more school children came aboard. In Nipomo, they met still other children who had arrived from Central City and Guadaloupe to the south. Now, for the first time in history, the children of San Luis Obispo and Santa Barbara Counties came together for the biggest play day that any of them had ever experienced. The little narrow-gauge was changing the lives of all of them, and there was more fun to come.

In May of that year, the parents of 16-year-old Anita Dana on the Los Berros por-

tion of the Nipomo Rancho, sent notes to numerous friends all over the county inviting them to their ranchita on Los Berros Creek to celebrate Anita's birthday. Two coaches on a special train left San Luis Obispo at 10 a.m. on May 17, "and after a pleasant run of a little over an hour, stopping at Arroyo Grande to take up a delegation bent on the same errand.." the train reached Nipomo. Over 150 people enjoyed the barbecue with Mexican dishes, wine and beer.

There was "music, singing..(and) dancing," the Tribune reported with "Mssrs. Williams and Albert Hartnell furnish(ing) the..music. Dancing was kept up until after daylight. At midnight an excellent supper was given and participated in by all. The whistle of the locomotive at about 8 o'clock in the morning notified the guests that the hour of departure had arrived."

Nearly every family in the area with ancestry dating from either the Mexican period or the early American period had joined in

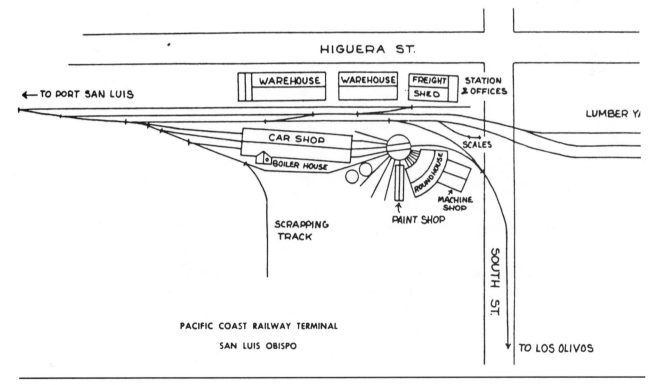

PACIFIC COAST RAILROAD *facilities originally located at Lower Higuera and South Streets.*

this celebration. There was something so magical and easy about riding on a train for a society accustomed to the bumps and jolts of horses and wagons.

The Queen of the Pacific, the company's new ship, arrived at Port Harford August 21, 1882 during her maiden voyage. After leaving Philadelphia with passengers, and "railroad iron and machinery for the San Luis Obispo and Santa Maria Railroad," the Queen had sailed to Rio de Janeiro and remained in port for seven days. Then, she had sailed the length of South America to the Strait of Magellan for the trip around the Horn. It took 10 days to navigate the Horn. She stayed at Valparaiso for eight days, taking on additional passengers before continuing her voyage north to California. Her time from Valpariso to Port Harford was 17 days, 4 hours, the fastest ever made by any commercial steamer.

All passengers stayed over in San Luis Obispo where they waited for the Orizaba to take them to San Francisco. The Queen unloaded her railroad supplies and equipment, remaining in port until the following Sunday when a railway excursion train with eight passenger cars took local people to Port Harford for a tour of the new vessel.

During a meeting of about 200 citizens at the Lytton Theater the next month, a resolution was passed requesting the Pacific Coast Steamship Company and the railroad to change the name of the landing from Port Harford to Port San Luis Obispo. John Harford had long since moved to San Francisco, so his

THE SEABIRD—Long before vessels could lay alongside wharves along the Central Coast, this vessel dropped anchor as close to shore as it dared, taking freight from lighters and passengers from surfboats.

ROUNDHOUSE— Pacific Coast narrow-gauge alongside engine stalls at the corner of Higuera and South Streets.

fame was fading in the area. But the company took no immediate action. However, one name change did occur. The narrow gauge railroad had been operating as two corporate entities for some years, one titled the San Luis Obispo and Santa Maria Railroad Company and the other the Pacific Coast Railway. In October, 1882, it became one legal entity to be known as the Pacific Coast Railroad.

By October ll, 1882, the company had completed track through Santa Maria to the Los Alamos Rancho. In anticipation of the railroad's arrival on the rancho a small subdivision of town lots had been laid out. The Los Alamos Hotel, later the Union Hotel, and a few other small businesses came into existence. The railroad also constructed a large warehouse for storing grain and other farm produce. This structure, restored, still stands.

Although excitement about the railroad gradually became less intense, groups still gathered to celebrate changes. For example, with the start of work to improve the line between the Port and Avila, a group of local women came out from San Luis Obispo to celebrate. Railroad Manager J. Millard Fillmore officiated while standing on a high bluff overlooking San Luis Obispo Bay. The group viewed Point San Luis on the southwest and Point Sal and Point Arguello to the distant south. It was a beautiful day. It was also soon apparent to all that they stood on one of the richest of Chumash Indian archeological sites, "a dwelling place and cemetery of the pre-historic Indian, whose long held sacred graves are now to be rudely thrown to the sea to make way for the iron road," a Tribune reporter wrote.

The honor of throwing the first shovel of soil was given to Mrs. H. H. Hays, wife of the area's late pioneer medical doctor. After the guests drank a toast to the success of the road, Ah Louis' Chinese laborers took up picks and shovels, and a search for Indian relics took place. Shells, flints, mortars, pestles, ollas and bones were exhumed. With arms full of treasures, the ladies later went down to the landing to watch the Barkentine William L. Beebee and two schooners unload freight at the wharf.

By now, Chauncey Hatch Phillips, entrepreneur extraordinary, had established the soundest reputation in the area for business acumen. He not only had been successful in the banking business, and had successfully promoted the needed stock sales for railway construction from the landing into

San Luis Obispo, but he had undertaken several land developments. During 1875, he had subdivided the Morro y Cayucos Ranchos where the coastal communites of Morro Bay and Cayucos are now situated. In 1882, while the Pacific Coast Railroad extended south, he worked with Edgar and Willis Steele in selling large parcels of land which they owned on four different Mexican land grants..the Arroyo Grande, the Bolsa de Chamisal, the Corral de Piedra and El Pismo, all located in southern San Luis Obispo County and all contiguous. The Steeles had purchased much of this land soon after the great drought in 1864 that destroyed so many herds of cattle and sheep in California. The value of this land had later increased many times and now its worth was further enhanced by the proximity of a railroad that could move agricultural products to the steamer port for shipment to city markets. The freight trains provided flag stops on every ranch of any size and maintained warehouses in every settlement that developed along the route.

Phillips and Charles Goodall, the president of the early Pacific Coast Steamship Company and the developer of the early railway, obviously became good friends. Phillips had actually traveled with Goodall in selecting the route of the railroad. In March, 1883, railroad manager J. Millard Fillmore again invited Phillips and a group of other local men to join Goodall in an "excursion" to Los Alamos. Since Goodall now had state authorization to build line all of the way to Santa Barbara, his arrival in town aroused much local interest.

The others traveling with Goodall included Manager Fillmore; John Dana of the Nipomo; E. B. Morriss, manager of the Cosmopolitan Hotel in San Luis Obispo; Isaac Goldtree of the Goldtree Bros. general store; Lew Warden, owner of a large breeding farm on the Canada de Los Osos; Judge William Beebee; and Myron Angel, now editor of the San Luis Obispo Tribune. They stopped at each station long enough to in-

UNTIL 1901, stagecoaches carried mail and passengers from the end of the line at Los Olivos to Santa Barbara. The trip took about 6 hours over San Marcos Pass.

spect the depots, grounds and warehousing facilities. They also gathered information about the crops and the financial prospects for the coming year. It was a dry season, and things did not look promising.

The steamship company was still losing freight business to herders who conducted cattle drives to market. Goodall let people know that both railroad and steamship freight rates had been reduced 30% for freighting mature live cattle to market and 50% for freighting calves. As an example of the capacity of the ships in the line to handle live freight, on March 25, 1883, the Orizaba loaded 800 live sheep on board. Five days later, the Ancon loaded 1500. One steamer, the Bonita, could take on a full cargo of exclusively live animals. Goodall wanted to encourage this business.

The Tribune told its readers: "At Los Alamos the party repaired to the Union Hotel..where a superb dinner..was waiting.

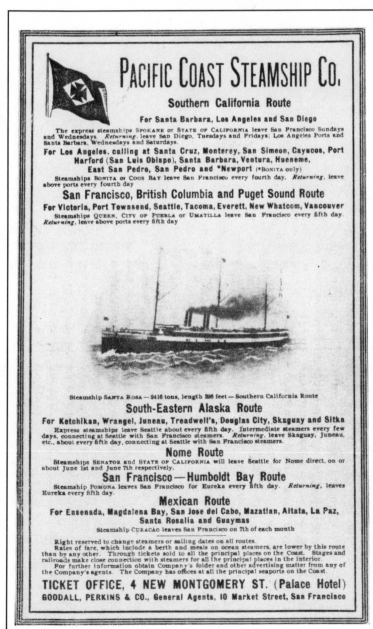

ABOVE: This old boxcar of the Pacific Coast Railroad, minus wheels, rests in Los Alamos near the company's old warehouses.

LEFT: This advertisement appeared in a turn-of-century issue of Sunset Magazine while the publication was still owned by Southern Pacific Railroad.

PACIFIC COAST Railroad storage building. Destroyed in 1988 to make room for a modern shopping complex.

Fat and tender roast turkey, succotash..excellent wines..." and a long list of other gourmet delights.

Myron Angel's History of San Luis Obispo County, published in 1883, said the Pacific Coast Railroad owned 64 miles of three-foot narrow gauge track. Company inventory included five locomotives, four passenger coaches, 120 platform cars, 20 box cars and 10 hand cars. Harford Wharf now extended 3000 feet into the bay and was 80 feet in width. It could accommodate the largest vessels sailing the Pacific Coast, and railroad track ran all of the way to the end of it. The wharf also included a warehouse and offices. Still, the federal government did not see fit to construct a breakwater.

During these years rumors continuously circulated about Southern Pacific Railroad plans to continue building track southward. Since 1873, Soledad had been the terminus of what would one day become the coastal line.

Chauncey Hatch Phillips had a way of investigating such rumors more thoroughly than most people of the county. He soon made a proposal to some of the principals of the Oregon Improvement Company, the holding company for the Pacific Coast Steamship Company and the Pacific Coast Railroad. These men had both the vision and the resources that made big enterprise possible. It is not surprising to find that they were responsive to Phillip's plan.

As a result, the West Coast Land Company came into existence March 26, 1886. Its immediate objective was the purchase, development and sale of large sections of land comprising ranchos El Paso de Robles, Santa Ysabel, the Eureka and the Huero Huero, a total of 64,000 acres. All of these properties were located in northern San Luis Obispo County above the Cuesta Pass.

George Perkins, who by now had served as governor of California (1880-1883), agreed to serve on the board of directors of the new corporation. John L. Howard, a principal in the Oregon Improvement Company, accepted the title of president. Isaac Goldtree, now a large landowner and a member of a wealthy merchant family in San Luis Obispo, became vice president and Robert E. Jack, owner of the 26,621-acre Rancho Cholame and a banker, was asked to serve as treasurer. Phillips reserved the position of secretary-manager of the company for himself. Now, he was set for the arrival of Southern Pacific at the northern end of the county.

In May, 1886, the San Luis Obispo Tribune reported 1500 Chinese coolies at work laying track out of Soledad. By July 20, the Southern Pacific was working across the King Ranch where the town of Kings (later King City) was laid out.

On October 1, 1886 a stringer for the Tribune who lived in the Estrella district a few miles east of San Miguel reported that he and his neighbors could hear heavy blasting. They assumed it was railroad construction. The big day occurred October 18, 1886. The first Southern Pacific train rolled into San Miguel, and people gathered from miles around for the celebration. The Tribune reported "that the town is full, too full for utterance, hardly equal to the occasion."

Southern Pacific reached the hot springs hotel settlement on the El Paso de Robles Rancho October 31, 1886. Construction of track continued south into the middle of the land purchased by the West Coast Land Company and there it stopped. Phillips had laid out a 160-acre site for a town which was, at first, named Crocker, but almost immediately changed to Templeton. Track was completed to Templeton on October 30, and the announcement of the arrival of the first work train occurred November 5, 1886. Templeton now became the new terminus for what would one day become the coastal line.

A great deal of uncertainly existed after Southern Pacific stopped construction. During an interview with a reporter in Los Angeles in June, 1887, Southern Pacific's

SOUTHERN PACIFIC reached San Luis Obispo May 5, 1894. Closed gap to Los Angeles in 1901. Pacific Coast Railroad lasted until 1940.

PRESIDENT JAMES MCKINLEY'S Special, May 10, 1901. This Southern Pacific presidential train stopped in San Luis Obispo where McKinley spoke at the Ramona Hotel.

President Leland Stanford said that the company now planned to lay track northward toward the coast from their valley line beginning at Saugus, then through Fillmore, Santa Paula and Ventura into Santa Barbara. "We expect to reach Santa Barbara in about three months," the manager accompanying Stanford said. "There is some heavy grading to be done along the beach, and it is a difficult road to build."

News about the first train reaching Santa Barbara from the south appeared in the San Luis Obispo Tribune on August 26. It was a reprint of an article from the Santa Barbara Press. The first train in town stopped at State Street, a short distance from the beach, and unloaded some 300 happy passengers. The Carpinteria brass band was on hand for the occasion, making the event even more festive. Horse-drawn buses and all three of the cities horse-drawn street cars transported guests to the heart of town.

It was time for the owners of the Pacific Coast Railroad to take another look at their long held plan to build narrow gauge track to Santa Barbara. The Southern Pacific

ENGINEER AND FIREMAN pose on Engine 101 that pulled President Theodore Roosevelt's car when he visited San Luis Obispo in 1906.

gap between Templeton and Santa Barbara was only about 125 miles. Southern Pacific surely intended to finish building track all of the way through to connect San Francisco and Los Angeles along the coast.

While these events were occurring, two men named Grover and Gates subdivided a long stretch of land between Arroyo Grande and the beach to the west, calling this new place Grover City. These same men also owned acreage on the John S. Bell ranch located to the west of Los Alamos. They planned to subdivide some of this land. Both of these sites were within the service area of the little Pacific Coast Railroad.

The owners of the Pacific Coast Railway soon made the decision to extend track from Los Alamos eastward into the Santa Ines Valley and lay out a town they called Los Olivos. In spite of the Southern Pacific, a small combine of investors thought they saw a chance to make money in land sales and the railroad expected to do well with freight and passenger service. By November 11, 1887, tracks were built. Chauncey Hatch Phillips, in charge of land sales, promoted Los Olivos far and wide. He placed advertising in newspapers all along the coast announcing a "grand excursion" and land auction for Wednesday, November 30, 1887.

Ben Brooks, now the new editor of the San Luis Obispo Tribune decided the Los Olivos event was one he should not miss, but he must have had some second thoughts when he awakened that morning, to find it raining.

He dressed for a wet day and walked to the train station on lower Higuera Street in San Luis Obispo. The first stop was Avila. To his amazement, steamers had arrived at Port Harford from both north and south loaded with passengers planning to take the narrow gauge to the Los Olivos development. They "paced the wet decks, balanced themselves against the bouncing billows, looked at the discouraging mist and rain." Some prospects, Brooks reported, gave up the whole notion of going ashore.

But most weathered the storm. Two engines pulled every available Pacific Coast passenger car. The cars were humid with so many wet people, crowded and uncomfortable. Many had to stand in the aisles. Some of the men squatted in place. Nearly all were growling unhappily. The railroad had intended to attach some open cars with temporary seats, but the weather precluded this action.

To his credit, Phillips had a temporary covered platform erected at the point where

STAGECOACH days in San Luis Obispo Country. From a painting by W. H. Hilton in 1876, now in the care of Wells Fargo Bank, San Francisco.

RAILROAD sequences for the film "Diamond Jim Brady" were filmed in San Luis Obispo and Santa Barbara Counties using rolling stock of the Pacific Coast Railroad. Star Edward Arnold poses on Engine 106, made over to resemble earlier engines.

the crowd debarked at Los Olivos. But, Brooks noted, "the soil at Los Olivos is deep and rich, and the plentiful moisture had readily penetrated it, so that the pedestrian could pick up a twenty-five foot lot on each foot in the course of a short walk."

Phillips had hired the San Luis Band to provide music, and although the fire smoked and sparked uncertainly in the rain, the delicious smells of barbecued meat tempted the crowd.

"There was a plentiful supply of bread and 'sack'..particularly 'sack,'" Brooks noted, and soon the crowd was in high spirits. People laughed and talked gaily, at least partially disregarding the rain.

Phillips took the stage and "palavered the congregation," helping them to see millions in the future city that was about to grow around them. H. W. Weller, an auctioneer from San Francisco, began his speech in advance of the offering. Colonel Seely,

AS THE PACIFIC Coast Railroad closed operations along the line, a group of rail fans and local citizens took one last excursion from San Luis Obispo to Avila. Here, some of them pose on the engine at San Luis Obispo.

working for the West Coast Land Company, stood as spotter so as not to miss a bid, and W. S. Hinkle set up a table to receive deposits and consummate land deals.

The first lots offered were those close to the depot. They were 50'x 140' in size and the bidding went as high as $300 for some of them.

Then a few lots down the proposed street near the site of the planned hotel were offered and sold. The foundation for the hotel had already been laid. A windmill was in place and water had been reached at 47 feet. T. W. Williams, who had established a lumber yard to serve prospective settlers, announced that he had thirty carloads of lumber ready for immediate sale.

J. W. Smith and P. B. Perfumo from San Luis Obispo bid extremely low on a number of properties, and much to everyone's amazement, they won their bids. They seemed prepared to continue bidding for every piece of land offered.

Phillips didn't like the way things were going. He didn't do anything about it immediately, but it became apparent that the whole Los Olivos development was going to be a disaster unless he took action. He finally gave the signal and all sales stopped. They had sold twenty-nine lots for about $6,300 that day.

The crowd moved to the tables for more food and drink. The mud grew deeper, the rain fell harder and everyone rushed for the train. People were very wet and sullen for the long ride back to San Luis Obispo and Port Harford.

All of the settlements along the Pacific Coast Railroad, including Los Olivos, were destined to develop slowly. Most of them remain small even today.

The Southern Pacific Railroad coastal line reached San Luis Obispo May 5, 1894, and the stock in the Pacific Coast Railroad fell to an all time low.

While most of the freight business of this central coast area gradually shifted to Southern Pacific Railroad, the Pacific Coast Steamship Company and the Pacific Coast Railroad continued operating. For many years the small line brought passengers and freight from the towns it served to its connection with Southern Pacific in San Luis Obispo. The mining of asphaltum and the discovery of oil in the area kept the railway alive for a while, but when the asphaltum was exhausted and the oil companies began piping their product, the little railroad went through a series of retrenchments. Line was built from Santa Maria to Betteravia to serve the sugar beet industry of the area, and they found other small industries to serve, but this business was not enough. Trucks could haul these products to the Southern Pacific connection in Guadaloupe or San Luis Obispo.

The Pacific Coast Railroad struggled into the new century, suffering $1 million in financial losses and finally stopping all service in 1940. Its last manager was the late Herbert C. Grundell, a lawyer and resident of San Luis Obispo. He oversaw the sale of the company's rolling stock, some of it to a small railroad in Hawaii. As shortages developed during World War II, the track was removed and sold for salvage to Dalien Steel Products Company in Los Angeles.

This little narrow gauge railroad had served a highly significant purpose during the last quarter of the nineteenth century in this coastal area. Railroad buffs still walk its route, gathering artifacts and mourning its loss. In recent years, a local group associated with the San Luis Obispo South County Historical Society has placed a monument at the location of the depot in each community the little railroad served.

OFF TO STEARNS WHARF and tea at the Potter Hotel on the beach at Santa Barbara.

AS WE COME TO THE END OF OUR HISTORIC POSTCARD JOURNEY...

...why not celebrate one more event. This formally dressed 1914 crowd joyfully dances to the waltzes and foxtrots of their time with music provided by an early wind-up Victrola, forbear to the high fidelity, stereo and electronic sounds of today.

How delightfully feminine our ladies appear with their plumed head dress, oriental fans and evening wear. And how elegantly suave the men look in black long-tailed jackets, stiff collars and bow ties.

In that year Victors and Victrolas ranged in price from $10 for the small oak model with horn speaker to $500 for the full size cabinet with record storage and dreamy Maxfield Parrish-type stamped paintings on the doors and sides.

Shall we dance one more dance, sing one more song, caress our lover one more time before the twenty-first century reels us into visits on other planets?

Thank You...

* Patricia Henley Nicholson, Mary Biaggini Hartzell, Donald Duncan, Eileen Kengel, Don Strassburg, Don and Mary Harrah, the late Hazel Hansen and the late Young Louis and so many others who shared their postcards and historical information with me.

* Armand Zolezzi for so generously commissioning this book.

* Bernice Loughran-Nicholson, my wife, for working out the cover design.

* Tomas Zazueta of ADCOM, whose new advanced desktop computing company produced the graphics for this book. He has much to offer people in the publications business.

* Editor George Brand of Senior Magazine for giving our idea a regular public forum by using our monthly old picture postcard feature stories.

* Special Collections Room, Cal Poly Library, for access to their growing collection of postcards, photos and original papers of the Central Coast.

* San Luis Obispo and Santa Barbara City-County Libraries for maintaining such excellent collections of archival materials, especially microfilmed publications of the Central Coast, for use by people like me.

Loren Nicholson

Loren Nicholson